John Cordy Jeaffreson, Christopher Jeaffreson

A Young Squire of the Seventeenth Century

John Cordy Jeaffreson, Christopher Jeaffreson

A Young Squire of the Seventeenth Century

ISBN/EAN: 9783337034436

Printed in Europe, USA, Canada, Australia, Japan

Cover: Foto ©ninafisch / pixelio.de

More available books at **www.hansebooks.com**

OF THE

SEVENTEENTH CENTURY.

FROM THE PAPERS (A.D. 1676-1686)

OF

CHRISTOPHER JEAFFRESON,

OF DULLINGHAM HOUSE, CAMBRIDGESHIRE.

EDITED BY

JOHN CORDY JEAFFRESON,

AUTHOR OF
"A BOOK ABOUT DOCTORS," "BRIDES AND BRIDALS," ETC.

IN TWO VOLUMES.

VOL. II.

LONDON:
HURST AND BLACKETT, PUBLISHERS,
13, GREAT MARLBOROUGH STREET.
1878.

All rights reserved.

CONTENTS

OF

THE SECOND VOLUME.

Part III.
(*Continued.*)

LONDON LETTERS.

CHAPTER III.

OFFICIAL NEWS AND REVELATIONS.

(17 November, 1682, to 17 December, 1682)

Measures against the Kidnabbers—Value of Convict Labour in St. Christopher's Island—Military Recruits for the Colony—Colonel Hill's Services and Distinctions—Mr. Blathwait's Services to the Colony—The Colonists advised to encourage Mr. Blathwait with Presents of Money—The Grant of Three Hundred Malefactors to the Colony—Mr. Brisborne, Secretary of the Admiralty—Colonel Legge, Lord Dartmouth—Colonel Hill's Departure for St. Christopher's Island . . . 3

CHAPTER IV.

TO THE KING IN COUNCIL.

(12 January, 1682-3.)

Charles Second's previous Grant to St. Christopher's. Nevis, Antigua and Mountserrat—The New Fort on Cleverly's Point—St. Kitt's—The Need of Military Munitions—H.M.'s Frigate, the 'Francis'—Loss of First Petition—Second Petition referred to the Lords of Trade 22

CHAPTER V.

GRAY'S INN AND THE CITY.

(17 January 1682-3, to 17 March, 1682-3.)

Care for Slaves—Gray's Inn Revells—Lord Dartmouth's Office in the Tower—Godwin Plantation, St. Kitt's—Soldiers for the West Indies—Failures in the City—Panic amongst the "Bankiers"—The Crown Tavern—Court News—Covent Garden Duellists—Outcry against Interlopers—The Writer's Contention with Captain Richardson—Sir Leoline Jenkins—A Scene in the Council Chamber—Bantam taken by the Dutch—Constantine Phipps migrates from Gray's Inn to the Temple 26

CHAPTER VI.

SPRING AND SUMMER.

(17 April, 1683, to 17 August, 1683.)

A Ludicrous Duel—Fire at Newmarket—A Gentlewoman marries a Butler—Old Books—Court Gossip—Edward Thorn's Misconduct—Health-Drinking at the Sun Tavern

—The Gaoler of Newgate again—His Influence with the Council—Bribes for Placemen—Emigrants to Carolina and Pennsylvania—A Steward's cruelty to Slaves—Constantine Phipps's Fine Qualities. . . . 51

CHAPTER VII.

PLANTER AND POLITICIAN.

(17 August, 1683, to September, 1683.)

A Faithless Steward.—Revolting Cruelty—Bad News from St. Kitt's—The Rye House Plot—Loyal Addresses to the King and Duke—Sir Charles Wheeler's Death—Duel between Colonel Nethway and Captain Billop—War declared by France against Holland and Spain—Mrs. Windall's Singing and Expertness on the Viol—West Indian Losses—The Writer's Mode of Life in the West Indies—Constantine Phipps at Worcester . 67

CHAPTER VIII.

AFTER THE PLOT.

(17 September, 1683, to 31 December, 1683.)

Relief of Vienna—Reported Capture of Gibraltar—Lord Dartmouth's Expedition—General Stapleton's Return—Loyal Addresses touching the Rye House Plot—Exchange News and Coffee House Gossip—Court and Town—Newmarket Races—The City and its Charter—Sir Henry Tulse—The Common Council—Lord William Russell and Algernon Sidney—Aaron Smith—Sir John Knight—The Captain General of the Leeward Islands—Intrigues for his Office. . . . 80

CHAPTER IX.

HARD WINTER AND COLD SPRING.

(January, February, March, 1683-4.)

Colonel Gamiell's Death—Sir Edward Brett's last Illness and Death—Small Pox in London—Turkey Tottering—European Politics—Negociations with Mr. Blathwait—Lady Russell's West Indian Friends—Apprehensions of War between England and France—Sir Nathaniel Johnson—The Spanish-Dutch Combination—Rye House Prosecutions—Captain Richardson's Extortions—The Thames Frozen Over—Frost Fair—A Fatal Season—Hardships at Sea—William of Orange—Governor Hill's influence—Mr. Sedgewick—The First Client. . 94

CHAPTER X.

THE HOT SEASON OF SIXTEEN SIXTY-FOUR.

(June, July, August and September, 1684.)

The Duke of York—A Military Demonstration—Sir Thomas Jenner—The Writer appointed Political Agent for St. Chistopher's Island—He presents a Congratulatory Address to the King and the Duke of York—Old Silver and New Plate—Extortions at Newgate—The Rogues' March from the Old Bailey to the River—Arms for the Malefactors—The Recorder's Triumph and the Gaoler's Victory—Three Partners in a curious Venture—Mrs. Lewis of Glamorganshire 115

CHAPTER XI.

DOMESTIC AND PUBLIC AFFAIRS.

(17 *September,* 1684, *to* 29 *October,* 1684.)

Edward Thorn's Misconduct—Constantine Phipps's Marriage—Sir Robert Sawyer, the Attorney-General—Lord-Keeper North—Sir Francis Withins—Chief Justice Jeffreys—Charles the Second and the Prince of Orange—Mr. Chidly—Van Bewmingen—The Bantam Claims—Siege of Buda—Lord Mayor Sir William Smith—Court Gossip—Religion and Loyalty in Fashion—Dejection of the Whigs—Imprisonment of Titus Oates . . 131

CHAPTER XII.

NEWS FOR THE PLANTERS.

(29 *October,* 1684, *to* 6 *December,* 1684.)

A Review on Putney Heath—Goodman the Player—Rosewell the Preacher—A Duel in a Play-House—Great Fire in the Temple—A great Fire at Powys House—Van Bewmingen and the Duke of Monmouth—The Bantam Claims—The Earl of Rochester—The Siege of Buda—Recent Appointments—A Talk of the Town—Official Changes—The Scotch Parliament—The Duke of York . 142

CHAPTER XIII.

THE CROWN PASSES.

(January and February, 1684-5

Rumours about Monmouth—Murder of Sir William Estcourt—Episcopal Changes—Constantine Phipps at the Bar—Official Appointments—Ambassadors to Foreign

Powers—Resistance to the Turk—Rumours of War—
Arrest of Colonel Danvers—Ministerial Honours—Scotch
Convicts for the West Indies—Charges against Patrick
Trant—Illness and Death of Charles the Second—James
the Second's Accession—A quick Voyage from the West
Indies—Charles the Second's Funeral—Restoration of
the White Staff Officers 161

CHAPTER XIV.

THE NEW REIGN.

(2 March, 1684-5 to April, 1685.)

Loyal Adresses to the New King—Edward Thorn's Dismissal—Transient Coldness between the Writer and Governor Hill—Another French Fleet—Sickness of the Horse Guards—Preparations for the Coronation and Opening of Parliament—The new Steward of the Writer's Plantations—A Second Shipment of Convicts and Arms for St. Christopher's Island—List and Particulars of the Malefactors 178

CHAPTER XV.

REBELLION.

(April, May, June, July, 1685.)

Another Rogue's March—Sir William Stapleton's Arrival
—A Loyal and Liberal Parliament—Sir James Russell's
Illness—Purchase of Negroes—Argyll's Rebellion—
Arrests in the West of England—The Western Rising—
The case of Lord Macclesfield and Mr. Fitton—Birth of
a Princess—Monmouth and Grey in London—The Duke's
Execution and Burial—Triumphal Return of the Guards
—New Levies—More Prisoners from the West—Disposal
of Regiments—Pursuit of Ferguson . . . 194

CONTENTS. xi

CHAPTER XVI.

THE LATE TROUBLES.

(August, 1685.)

West Indian Markets—Peter De Grave's Death—Argyll's Rising—His Execution—Monmouth's Insurrection—Military Movements—Facts not published in the Gazettes—The Battle of Bridgewater—The Earl of Arlington, Lord Chamberlain—The Earl of Feversham—The Lords Stamford, Delamere and Brandon in the Tower—Changes in the Army—The Duke of Albemarle—Lord Churchill—Ensign Matthew—Gaols full of Rebels—St. Christopher's Island asking for a Cargo of Rebels . . 213

CHAPTER XVII.

PERSONAL AFFAIRS.

(17 September, 1685, to 17 November, 1685.)

Mrs. Lewis of Glamorganshire and Channell Row—Edward Thorn's preposterous Misconduct—Thames Water—The Treaty of Neutrality—Impudent Demands—Severity needful in governing Slaves—Escape of a Convict—The Writer's anxiety about Captain Foster—Countenance afforded by the Writer's Friends to his knavish Steward—Dilapidation and barenness of the Writer's House in St. Kitts 227

CHAPTER XVIII.

BUSINESS AND POLITICS.

(9 December, 1685, to 18 January, 1685-6.)

An Absent Partner—A Liberal Parliament—Sir William Stapleton and the Lords Commissioners—Pardons for Refusing the Test—Lord Anglesey's Indictment of Bernard Howard—Trial of Charles Gerard, Lord Gerard of Brandon—Lord Delamere, Sir Robert Cotton and Mr. Offley out on Bail—Amsterdam and the Prince of Orange—West Indian Morals—The Royal African Company—The French Fleet—Fire at Wapping—Bills of High Treason—Religious Persecution in France . . 241

CHAPTER XVIII.

LONDON AND THE LEEWARD ISLANDS.

(*January,* 1685-6.)

Impolitic Severity—The Committee for Trade—Alderman Lucy—Alderman Jefferys—Colonel Byar—West Indian Politics—Trial of Lord Delamere in Westminster Hall—Mr. Hambden guilty of Treason—Episcopal Changes—The Demand for the Principality of Orange—Madam Sydley, Countess of Dorchester—The Writer's reason for holding his West Indian Property in his own Hands—Anticipation of Civil Troubles—A Store opened at the Writer's House in St. Kitt's. . . . 253

CHAPTER XIX.

WESTMINSTER AND THE WEST INDIES.

(28 *January,* 1685-6, *to* 2 *March,* 1685-6.)

Sir William Stapleton's Health—The Queen's bitterness against the Countess of Dorchester—Lord Dartmouth—Changes and Rumours at Court—Chit-Chat—The King's Frugality—Sufferings of Voyagers—Homage rendered to the Countess of Dorchester—Legal Promotions—Lord Northampton's Disappointment—Duels and Duellists in High Life—The Duke of Grafton's Reappearance at Court—His Duel with Mr. Talbot . . . 264

CHAPTER XX.

THE LATEST NEWS.

(2 *March*, 1685-6, *to* 4 *June,* 1686.)

The Parson of Woppenham—Legal Rumours—Illness of the French King—French Protestants—Religious Persecution in Piedmont—The Camp on Hounslow Heath—French Designs on the Plate Fleet—Official changes in Ireland—Religious Animosities in London—Storms at Sea—Constantine Phipps settled at Fulham—An unsettled Account—Distress of the French Refugees—Charitable Relief of the Sufferers—The Fall of the Bull Inn 277

CHAPTER XXI.

TATTLE OF THE CLIQUES.

(4 June, 1686, *to* 8 *September,* 1686.*)*

The Court at Windsor—Prorogation of Parliament—Sale of White Servants—Gifts to Colonial Governors—The Duke of Albemarle, Governor of Jamaica—Sir Edmund Andrews—The King's Treatment of the Navy—The New Ecclesiastical Commission—A Duel at Epsom—The New Privy Councillors—Sir William Stapleton's Death—Lady Stapleton's Troubles—Token Drinking at the Exchange Tavern—Proceedings against the Bishop of London—The Siege of Buda—Siege of Hamburgh by the Danes 292

CHAPTER XXII.

THE LAST LETTERS OF THE FOURTH YEAR IN LONDON.

*(*8 *September,* 1686, *to* 16 *September,* 1686.*)*

A Royal Progress—Trial of the Bishop of London by the Ecclesiastical Commissioners—Dr. Sharp, Rector of St. Giles's in the Fields—Arguments of Counsel and the Sentence—Refusal of the Bantam Claims—Lady Stapleton and the French Priests—Constantine Phipps on the Welsh Circuit—Health-Drinking at Cambridge Assizes—Capture of Buda—Mrs. Sarah Gordon of Goodman's Fields—Advice to Lieutenant Munday—Sir Nathaniel Johnson's Preparations for a Voyage to the Leeward Islands. 309

Part III.

(*Continued.*)

LONDON LETTERS.

CHAPTER III.

OFFICIAL NEWS AND REVELATIONS.

(17 *November*, 1682, *to* 17 *December*, 1682).

Measures against the Kidnabbers—Value of Convict Labour in St. Christopher's Island—Military Recruits for the Colony—Colonel Hill's Services and Distinctions—Mr. Blathwait's Services to the Colony—The Colonists advised to encourage Mr. Blathwait with Presents of Money—The Grant of Three Hundred Malefactors to the Colony—Mr. Brisborne, Secretary of the Admiralty—Colonel Legge, Lord Dartmouth—Colonel Hill's Departure for St. Christopher's Island.

LETTER XIV.

To Ensign Edward Thorn, the Writer's agent and steward on St. Christopher's Island.

[*Note.*—From the writer's estimate of the market-value in the Leeward Islands of a malefactor, bound to serve his buyer for eight years, the reader may form a fair conception of the profits made by the exporters of malefactors to the plantations, and the yet greater profits made by the kidnappers who paid nothing for their livestock to commissioners, secretaries, recorders, and underlings. If we take the lower of the two rates at which the writer computes the worth of an average convict for eight years, *i.e.*, 2,200 lbs. of sugar, or £13 15*s*. 0*d*. of money, we find that the gross value of 300 malefactors would be £4,125; from which sum we must deduct £1,500 for cost of transport. The exporters would therefore have taken on the lot of labourers £2,625, equal to about £13,125 of money at its present worth; had not extortionate officials, from courtly secretaries like Mr. Blathwait, and grave judges like the Recorder of London, down to the gaolers and turnkeys of gaols, insisted on having a share in the spoil. It should, however, be borne in mind that the exporters of convicts were liable to heavy forfeitures if any of the convicts should escape; and that having been paid in sugar or other produce, they sometimes sustained losses in converting the com-

modity into money in the London market.—
J.C.J.]

London, 25 November, 1682.

Ensign Thorn.—In the enclosed long letter of the sixteenth instant, I have made no mention of the silver-hilted sword, designed for Mr. John Matthews, according to whose order I have sent one so like mine owne, that I feare he will thinke it the same. But I can assure you otherwise. For I keepe my owne sworde and handle for my owne weare, so soon as I come out of mourning. I hope it will please the young gentleman so well, that he will not grudge to give a hogshead of sugar in casque for it. I pray, sende me what you can for it.

The traders to the West Indies in general, and more especially the Jamaica merchants, being much dissatisfied with the great discouragement given by the Lord Chief Justice Pemberton to the sending servants to these parts, some of the principall persons, as Colonell Byer, Sir Peter Colleton, Colonel Thornbury, with many others, were to wait upon his lordeship about it, and have since moved the King and council in it; by whom it was referred to the Lords of the Committee, who referred it again to the Lord Chief Justice North.

The same day that the Lords of the Committee had a hearing of that businesse, which was Saturday last, I moved their lordships for a grant of 300 malefactors, by a petition, which I drew upon that day, being incouraged to take that opportunity. And it succeeded not amisse. For the Lord President promised me, that they would recommend it to the government, that the malefactors might serve eight yeares, which is double the tyme that others have used to serve; for *that* you must know was one part of the Prayer of my Petition, that thereby the islanders may thinke it reasonable to advance the prices, for the incouragement of those that should be at the charge and trouble of sending malefactors over, which are greater than ever I could imagine, (considering his Majesties grant of 40*s.* per head) besides the hazard of the great security to be given. For I finde the prison keepers will have a fee underhand, or else nothing is to be done. But provided the act for the taking of servants be removed, and an addition made that those who are shipt as malefactors, shall serve eight yeares, and be sould at 22 or 2400 per head, payment being to be made by the same ship, I thinke Captain Hill and I shall undertake it; the Lords of the Committee having accepted our offer, and granted an order to us, which we may take out when we finde occasion. If ever anything comes of it, I shall give you an accompt by name, which of them I thinke best for the plantation; and you may informe yourself of the master of the ship, how they do behave themselves in the voyage. But I give you advice beforehand, that you must never expect to take up any on my accompt, but what you can purpose to pay for as others do by the same ship. If the hurricanes are as bad this year as last, you will be almost forced to plant indigo, to keep the wolf from the door. Of which poore weed I have reassumed so good an opinion that, if upon a small tryal, made by you upon the upper land, you and I finde that it turns to a good accompt, I shall, if you think fit, treat with you about buying a parcel of negroes and servants, and we will try our fortunes together for a few yeares. You see that the charge I am at in what I send, together with John Holcroft's passage, amounts to very near one hundred and sixty pounds sterling; besides the charge I am at for the public of the islands. I hope the effects will be best evidence of my care and diligence in those concernes.

The 23rd instant, I tooke the order obteyned for thirty men to be sent as recruits in the Deptford ketch, which I immediately carried to the Lords Commissioners of the Treasury, and made friends to get it read; upon which it was ordered that the Lieutenant of the Tower should attend upon them this morning; when I am to wait to know what the issue of it will be. . . . . .

Your affectionate friend,
CHRISTOPHER JEAFFRESON.

LETTER XV.

To Captain James Phipps, a planter on St. Christopher's Island. Dated from London, 2 December, 1682.

The greater part of this long letter sounds the praises of Captain Hill, the newly-appointed Governor of the island, who has completely won the writer's good opinion. The Captain has seen service in France and Flanders, as well as in England, " where he bears the commission of eldest lieutenant of horse, as well as of Brigadier of the Duke's Guards." His rank in the army, therefore, is higher than that of any other officer serving under General Stapleton. The gentleman's " courage is undoubted, and yet he is free from pride; he is affable, courteous, and of a very good disposition." He will be found in the West Indies, as he has been found at home, "a trew and loyall Protestant, a stout soldier, and an honest, trew heart." Having thus enlarged on the Captain's merits, the writer sets forth the steps he has taken to furnish the island with malefactors, bound to serve eight years, who will be far more worth 2,400 lbs. of sugar each, than malefactors bound to serve only four years, are worth 1,800 lbs. of sugar each, at which price the islanders have been glad to buy such cattle. In conclusion, the writer says, "The enclosed letters I received of our brother Constantine. I saw him dance at the revels at Grays Inn, where he was the second or third best dancer of the eight which were the revellers permitted to dance. The Master of the revels is knighted, and the revellers escaped it very narrowly. The bearer of this letter knows not its contents, nor one worde of it. Therefore there can be no design of flattering him or abusing you. Far be either from me." The bearer of this epistle was the exemplary Captain Hill himself.

LETTER XVI.

To Captain Willett, a planter on St. Christopher's Island.

[*Note.*—The omitted parts of this letter consist of statements concerning the recruits and malefactors, identical in substance with announcements set forth in previous pages, and of commendations of Captain Hill, the bearer of the epistle, who is of course ignorant of its contents. The advice that the islanders should make a present to Mr. Blathwait is a noteworthy example of the corruption prevalent in official circles in the seventeenth century. What would be now-a-days thought of the Colonial Secretary who should accept and look for secret gifts of money from every colony having need of his assistance? What would any such Secretary think of the political agent of a British dependency who would fain conciliate him by slipping a note for £100 into his hand? It should be observed that whilst he calls the fees to gaolers *bribes*, the writer regards the bribes paid to the Secretary for Foreign Plantations as "presents."—J. C. J.]

London, 2 December, 1682.

Sir.—Upon my first arrival at London, I deferred no tyme to wait on Mr. Blathwait with the Generall's letter, and other papers. And so from tyme to tyme, I took several occasions to wait on him, and to discourse him in the matters relating to our islands. He told me at first that the recruits for the companys would be hardly obteyned at this time. I proposed the facility of sending them in some of his Majesties ships, bound for those parts; but he still persuaded me to deferre the delivery of my petition until he should give me notice of some king's ship, ordered that way, which I looked upon as the most suitable occasion to tyme my business in. For it has been my care, and shall be, to be watchfull not to slip any opportunity, by which I may be capable of rendering any service to the public of the island of St. Christopher; *whom, were I worthy to advise, it should be to make this Esquire Blathwait their friend by some present, for he is in a station that enables him to be one, and such incouragements might induce him to be willing, to doe kindnesse to vs, when we shall have occasion to make vse of him.* I must confesse he haith been more kind, than I could expect, in assisting Captain Hill and me in our businesse; and though the recruits now obteyned are but small in comparison of our wants, yet it is to be hoped more will follow. For it appears by the order that notice is taken that the General requires eighty or a hundred, of which these are sent as a part. It is well we had them drawne out of the standing regiments of the guard. They are much better soldiers than new men raised out of the scum of the towne. They will come well-clothed and armed.

The order upon my petition for the 300 malefactors we have not yet taken out. For, upon search made by vs in the gaols, wee find very few men, and *those* not worth sending. And we find that they are to be delivered to us out of no other prisons than London and Middlesex; so that it will take up some tyme to ship off the full complement, because 300 men are not condemned in one or two counties in two or three years tyme. The keepers of the prisons oppose vs, and must be bribed. But the great impediment in our way is the security required that none shall escape or returne within the term of eight years, for which they are to serve. The returne I don't fear so much as the escape, before we can get them on board, or before they are clear of land. At 1800 lbs. ahead it is not worth the while, the hazard, and the trouble. . . . . . .

Your most faithful friend and servant.

CHRISTOPHER JEAFFRESON.

Postscript.—If the country should think it convenient to present Mr. Blathwait, I would not seek to draw them into great expenses, but, as was formerly proposed twenty-pounds or thereabouts, and as we finde the effects of that, to do more as occasion may require.

[*Note.*—There is something droll as well as startling in this cool and wary proposal to bribe an important officer of the State with moderate bribes, following one another at intervals,—to administer corruption by instalments, and regulate the doses by nice observation of the results of the treatment. Now we know his secret practice, it is no longer surprising that Mr. Blathwait had an income of £2,000 a year.—J. C. J.]

LETTER XVII.

To Captain Pogson, a planter on St. Christopher's Island. Dated from London, 30 November, 1682.

Commending Captain Hill to Captain Pogson's friendly regard; and urging that the price of malefactors should be raised, and other steps taken so that merchants in England may be encouraged to furnish the island with an adequate supply of white labourers. Captain Hill (described as a man "very well beloved and having a great number of good as well as great friends about court") is said to have exerted himself in vain to have obtained a reduction of security (of £100 for every man) for the safe custody throughout eight years of the three hundred malefactors. Touching Mr. Secretary Blathwait's services, the writer observes, "I could wish that every one in our island were as willing as I to contribute (every man according to his capacity) towards a gratuity to Mr. Blathwait, which would be a justice to him, and a kindnesse to ourselves. He is able to repay vs sevenfolde, it lyeing in his way to render more service to that island, than it may be its inhabitants are aware of, as occasions shall present."

LETTER XVIII,

To General Sir William Stapleton, Captain-General of the Leeward Islands.

London.

Sir.—According to your Excellencies directions, I made an application to the Lords of the Committee for the three hundred malefactors; requesting by my petition that they might be ordered to serve double the time of other servants, that is to say eight years, which was so well represented that the Lord President, tould me it should be recommended to the government.

In the meantyme Captain Hill and I shall have an order for the delivering them to vs, upon our giving in security, that none of them shall escape, or retourne in the tyme limited.

I am sorry the recruits to be sent are so farre short of the number that your Excellency proposed to their Lordships, to supply the vacancies in the companys. But they are good men, drawne out of his Majesties own regiment of guards. They are to be cloathed and well armed, and to have their arreares payd them, before they part hence, which will hardly be before Christmasse; by reason it was ordered at first that the 'Deptford Ketch' should transport them; but since that, the 'Francis,' a sixth-rate frigate, of about a hundred and fourty or fifty tuns, is appointed. She will carry sixteen or eighteen guns, and forty-five men. Captain Charles Carlisle has a commission to command her.

I find that, unless your Excellency will be pleased to make use of your authority to summon the Islands to the speedy payment of Captain Jory's bond, and the discharge of the security, it is in a likelyhood of continueing in the same condition that it has been for four years; the debts will be augmented with interest to the certain and unnecessary prejudice of the islands, if not to the detriment of the security for the several islands. So, I hope you will likewise please to see them discharged. The compassing of which work lying wholly in your Excellency's power,

I humbly offer it to your consideration to judge of the reasonableness of the thing. I shall not trouble your Excellency for this tyme with anything more than the payment of my duty, with my most humble service to your Excellency and your lady, by the hands of Captain Hill, who can give a further and better account of all occurrences and matters, relating to public affairs, as well as of those relating to the islands under your Excellency's government, than I am able to do, and especially whilst at this distance. Therefore I take leave for the present, remaining as ever Your Excellency's
 Most faithful and unfeigned humble
  servant to command,
   CHRISTOPHER JEAFFRESON.

Postcript.—I pray, present my humble remembrances to Sir James Russell and his lady, and to Captain Jory and his lady.

[In connection with this letter, it may be observed that it is followed immediately in the Letter Book by a copy of the Official Minute of the proceedings at the Court at Whitehall, touching the petition of the Captain-General of the Leeward Islands for eighty or one hundred soldiers on St. Christopher's Island, when it was ordered by His Majesty and Council that thirty well-equipped soldiers should be sent to that island in the 'Deptford Ketch;' together with two other copies of Orders, by the King and Council, for the transport and equipment of the same soldiers. Marginal notes to these two last-named copies, show — that Christopher Jeaffreson (as the political agent of the Leeward Islands in the matter) delivered one of these orders to "Mr. Brisborn (*i. e.* Brisbane), Secretary to the Commissioners of the Admiralty on 7th December at about noon;" and that he delivered the other of the two orders on the 14th of December to "Colonel Legge, the now Lord Dartmouth, at his office in the Tower, according to appointment." John Evelyn speaks of Mr. Brisbane as a learned, industrious and agreeable man. Samuel Pepys refers to George Legge, created Lord Dartmouth in 1682.—J. C. J.)

LETTER XIX.

To Ensign Edward Thorn, the Writer's agent and steward in St. Christopher's Island. Dated from London, 2 December, 1682.

Insisting on the merits of Captain Hill, the bearer of the letter, who is again represented as a man of good military reputation and strong connections at Court. Ensign Thorn is strenuously enjoined to offer every attention in his power to the captain and his lady, on their first arrival in the island. The writer refers to his exertions for St. Kitt's, in respect to the recruits and malefactors. With regard to European news, of which there is a dearth, he says, "The Intelligencers have laid down their arms, whether in submission to authority, as some report, or through a want of subject matter, to make their impertinent pamphlets vendible, I am doubtful; but so it is that nothing but a gazette, one quarter stuft up with advertisements, is twice a week produced by the press; by which there is little else to be understood but that the Emperor of Germany, betweene the two potent armies threatening his territories with a heavy warr on both hands, so soon as the season will permit, is endeavouring to make peace with either or both; though as yet his endeavours that way have met with small hopes of successe. No man knows what the issue may be."

CHAPTER IV.

TO THE KING IN COUNCIL.

(12 *January*, 1682-3).

Charles Second's previous Grant to St. Christopher's, Nevis, Antigua and Mountserrat—The New Fort on Cleverly's Point—St. Kitt's—The Need of Military Munitions—H.M.'s Frigate, the 'Francis'—Loss of First Petition—Second Petition referred to the Lords of Trade.

LETTER XX.

The Writer's Petition to His Majesty Charles the Second, for iron, cannon, shot, arms and ammunition, for the new Fort now under course of erection on Cleverly's Point in St. Christopher's Island.

To the King's most excellent Majesty. The humble Petition of Christopher Jeaffreson

Showeth, that whereas your Majesty hath been graciously pleased, for the incouragement and forwarding of the several fortifications in and upon the islands under the Government of his Excellency, Sir William Stapleton, to order fifteen hundred pounds to be distributed by four equal portions to the islands of St. Christopher, Nevis, Antegoa and Mountserrat; which seasonable and Royal Assistance of your Majesty to your poor subjects, the inhabitants of the island of St. Christopher hath so farre incouraged them in their great undertaking of erecting a strong fort upon Cleverly's Poynt in the sayd island, (more regular, and for bignesse and strength as well as situation much more considerable, than any other fortification upon any of those your Majesty's Leeward Islands), that in a short tyme it may be made a safe and defensible retreat to your Majesty's subjects in case of extremity, and at all tymes a defense and security to the Road where most ships, trading to that island, usually anchor;—but forasmuch as cannon, shott, armes and ammunition are extreamly wanted in the sayd fort, and the inhabitants by meanes of their more than ordinary charges in building and making the same, are altogether incapable of furnishing the sayd fort therewith; the armes and ammunition for the militia being provided at the cost of the particular inhabitants.

Therefore your Petitioner humbly prays your Majesty to take into your Royal consideration the condition and wants of the sayd fort on St. Christopher's Island; that what iron, cannon and shot, your Majesty shall be graciously pleased to spare, and also, such armes and ammunition as your Majesty shall see convenient to allow, may with the lesse charge be transported in the 'Francis,' one of your Majesty's frigates, now ordered for that island. And your petitioner as in duty bound shall ever pray, &c., &c.,

[*Note*.—To the copy of this petition in the Letter-Book are attached the two following notes in the petitioner's hand-writing:— (1) "This petition was delivered to Mr. Blathwait to be read at a meeting of the King and Council on the 22nd of December but was not read, but referred to the next meeting;" (2) "12 Jan. 1682-3 Mr. Blathwait having lost the above petition, I drew another in the same words, except some alterations towards the latter end, and a little in the prayer of it, which last petition was delivered and read in Council this 12th of January 1682, and was referred to the Lords of the Committee for Trade."

CHAPTER V.

GRAY'S INN AND THE CITY.

(17 *January* 1682-3, *to* 17 *March* 1682-3.)

Care for Slaves—Gray's Inn Revells—Lord Dartmouth's Office in the Tower—Godwin Plantation, St. Kitt's—Soldiers for the West Indies—Failures in the City—Panic amongst the "Bankiers"—The Crown Tavern—Court News—Covent Garden Duellists—Outcry against Interlopers—The Writer's Contention with Captain Richardson—Sir Leoline Jenkins—A Scene in the Council Chamber—Bantam taken by the Dutch—Constantine Phipps migrates from Gray's Inn to the Eemple.

LETTER XXI.

To Ensign Edward Thorn, the Writer's agent and steward in St. Christopher's Island. Dated from London, 1 February 168¾.

Giving directions for the management of the writer's plantations, and urging the steward to write at great length of the affairs

of the island. Regretting the brevity of
Ensign Thorn's last letter, the writer says,
"You would have been kind in informing
me how the work of our fort and the
magazines have been carried on, since I
left the island. This might have been
useful to me, and perhaps advantageous to
the public of the island." Reference is
made to Captain Snow's last run from the
West Indies to London, who "was but a
month in his passage from the islands to
the soundings, but was afterwards three
weekes beating off the chops of the
Channel, before the windes would admit
him." Respecting the slaves, the writer
says, "I am glad I have sent you some
medicinal drugs, which I fear will be
wanted amongst the negroes, after their
unwholesome dyet. I pray, be careful of
them. Use Carduus' posset with a dose of
mithridate or Venice treacle upon the
coming on of the distempers; but spend not
your private store to spare the doctor, who
you know must be paid for it. But I have
sent those necessaries that my people may

have medicine much oftener then the chyrurgion would be willing to furnish those necessary druggs."

LETTER XXII.

To Captain James Phipps, a planter, at St. Christopher's Island.

[*Note.*—One of the several epistles, in which the writer intimates how much more useful he could be to the island, if he were its formally accredited Political Agent, this letter exhibits some of the services required of such an officer, and affords some curious illustrations of the way in which petitioners were treated by the Circumlocution offices of Charles the Second's time.— J. C. J.]

London, 1 February, 168$\frac{2}{3}$.

Dear Brother.—I have troubled you with severall letters (if received) since I arrived, and would not omit any opportunity of saluting you with my most humble services. Our good brother Constantine and I often drink your health; and especially we did so the other day, when he delivered me the enclosed. He talked of writing himself, but for this time you will do charitably in accepting of his love and excusing him; for that it is term tyme, and moreover the revelling, to which his Majesty was invited, and the preparations for Candlemas day are very lawful excuses. I am labouring to doe something for our island, tho' it be a little against the hair, for a private person to act in a public concern unless otherwise capacitated than I am. But when I found that the presenting the Lords of the Committee with a view of the plat of our fort and its wants, and the being referred to the Lord of Dartmouth, after long attendance produced little or no effect, I proceeded to petition the king and council for cannon, shot, armes, and ammunition for the fort. The first petition was lost; the second I preferred was read, and by order referred to the Lords of the Committee. This order cost me two-and-fifty shillings and sixpence, before I could get it to Sir Phillip Lloyd's clerk; and it produced nothing but another reference to the Lord of Dartmouth. I made my application twice or thrice to his lordship, who tould me, *if we could find money he would find all we wanted.* I was no stranger to such rubs. I had received several, and I could not well expect better; whilst I am cautious how I lavish out more money than is absolutely necessary, being so far from having any assurance of being reimburst, that I am doubtful whether I shall receive thanks, and not be laughed at for my paynes. However, according to his lordship's order, I waited upon him at his office in the Tower, (he being Master of the Ordnance) and there the plat of the fort being again produced before his lordship and his assistants, I again declared its wants, and had the liberty of some discourse, being asked several questions concerning it and our stores. There were one or two mathematicians that found fault with the eastermost part of it, and that it was so small; all which was easily answered and in the main it was very well approved of, considering it was in those parts. The Lord of Dartmonth ordered me to attend at the next council day, for that he designed then to make his report concerning it. But Mr. Blathwait hath much discouraged me, at least from the hopes of anything but some iron guns for the present; moneys being extream scarce, and the disfurnishing of the king's store now being looked upon as money out of purse, which comes very slowly. The next Council day, I attended from ten to twelve, to no purpose. I must waite their leisure, and shall not grudge at it, provided it is successful. Thus I have troubled you with a short account of my proceedings in behalfe of our island, which I pray God to prosper. . . . . .

CHRISTOPHER JEAFFRESON.

LETTER XXIII.

To the Writer's beloved friend Captain Pogson, a planter of St. Christopher's Island. Dated from London, 20 February, 168$\frac{2}{3}$.

Having received information as to the unsoundness of Mr. Du Shambray's title to the Godwin Plantation in the island, which property, together with the negroes, horses and cattle upon it, Captain Freeman is sanguine of recovering by suit of law; and knowing that

Captain Pogson thinks of purchasing the property, the writer hastens to warn his friend not to throw away his money on a bad title. The writer's information on this matter has been obtained from Mr. Blathwait at the office of Foreign Plantations and from Captain Freeman himself, which last-named gentleman sanctions the communication.

LETTER XXIV.

To Captain Hill, Deputy Governor of St. Christopher's Island.

[*Note.*—The reader should not miss this letter's account of the stir and panic in the city on the occasion of the failure of "Temple, a bankier in Lumbard Street."— J. C. J.]

London, 27 February, 168⅔.

Honoured Sir.—I have some reason now to hope that what I have been so long soliciting will be at last effected. Mr. Blathwait tells me that my lord of Dartmouth intends to make a favourable report to the Lords of the Council upon the merrits of my petition, referred to him by them. I went several tymes to wait upon his lordship about it; and he seemed to resent the businesse very well. I was advised not to be too pressing in it; and I found there was not that occasion, as I supposed. For the 'Frances' frigate is so deep loaden with provisions and necessaries, that I fear the thirty men will be but verry ill-accommodated. There is so little room for cannon, and what I expected would have been sent in her to St. Christopher's, that Captaine Carlile seemes perplexed, where to stow the armes of the thirty men, whom I pity, poor souls. I fear they will be pestered, so that their health and lives will be endangered by it. I was yesterday at the Tower, to discourse Captain Cheeke about it, but I could not meete with him. Captain Carlile carries (as he tells me) three yeares provision for his shippe; he being appointed to creuse so long about those islands.

The affaires of Europe are in a very unsettled condition; for the year is far spent, and the King of France (who, it is certain, cannot lay still) will in a short tyme be in action; but with whom he will make war or peace is most doubtfull.

We continue here much after the same rate, and in the same condition you left vs in; which you know was none of the best, and the prospect of amendment is very small. Last weeke, one Temple, a bankier in Lumbard Street shut vp shop. The cause of his misfortune, is by common report, layd at the Lord Moulgrave's door, who, it is sayd, was so outragious in his eager demands of twelve or fifteen thousand pounds, which he had in the sayd Temple's hands, that not onely the neighbours, but most of the creditours, tooke notice of it. However, my lord got £5,000 of his money; and to-morrow, it is sayd, proposals will be made at the Crowne Tavern, behind the Exchange, to all the creditours. But it is whispered as if there were more bankiers in the same condition, tho' they keepe open doors yet. But the whole credit of the nation is dwindling. It is feared the Chamber of London will never recover its credit. The East India Company are much suspected.

The interlopers are stopt; and money is a scarce commodity throughout the kingdome.

Now all that I can say as to businesse is that I have been with Captain Richardson several tymes; and yesterday he tould me, that this weeke there will be a general pardon granted, and then we shall know what men may be had; and I will lose no tyme in it; for there are one or two ships now almost ready to sayle for the Leeward Islands, viz.,—Captain Bowman and Captain John Lawrence. By the last, I would, if possible, send the malefactors.

The Court is removing, in a few days, to Newmarket. There is no news stirring. I pray present my sister's and my service to your good lady. . . . . .

      Christopher Jeaffreson.

LETTER XXV.

To Ensign Edward Thorn, the Writer's agent and steward in St. Christopher's Island.

[*Note*.—The writer's anticipation of trouble with Captain Richardson about prison fees payable on the delivery of malefactors, and the measures taken against two interlopers in the river Thames, are amongst the more interesting points of this letter. The unpublished portions of the letter relate to the departure and course of ships for the West Indies, and trivial matters touching the writer's plantations.—J. C. J.]

London, 1 March, 168¾.

Ensign Edward Thorn.—...... Captain Bowman tells me he shall sayle this week, and Captain John Lawrence by the tenth of March, in whom I have all along designed to send what malefactors I can get. I suppose that the pardon will be out this week; and till then I cannot know what may be done in it. Besides, I must expect some opposition from Captain Richardson, when he knows upon what ground I go. For I know he will expect the prison fees from me, and will be very loath to part with them, until he is payd the fees.

I send you this by Captain Charles Carlile, commander of the 'Frances' frigate, which carries over the thirty men to recruit the two companies. He bears the character of a stout and diligent officer. He is young, and this is the first voyage he ever went captain. I wish him better luck than any of his predecessors. Captain Billop talkes very high still. He is newly freed from a scurvy dilemma he was in about the killing of one Mr. Glover; which, it seemes, was done by one Lashly, with Captain Billop's sword in Covent Garden. Lashly was condemned, but pardoned by the King; and Captain Billop was acquitted at the Sessions last Wednesday; but, I believe, not without some cost. But now he discourses as if he would do strange things, against those, I suppose, that have little reason to fear him.

He will scarce allow any honest man to live in the Leeward Isles, besides Colonel Williams and Captain Pogson—that is of his acquaintances. He is a professed enemy of all sorts of interlopers, and declares himself to be such publickly. It is certainly no small oversight in the Royal Company and other companies, that are infected with interlopers, not to procure a commission for him, who is so ready to scour the seas of these their adversaries.

But seriously the interlopers have met a check in the river; for, having taken courage from their successe in former enterprises, they have not feared to speake their designes so publickly, that in my opinion they have drawn upon themselves the troubles they are in.

The first was Captain Sands, a man of great concernes, bound for the East Indies; the most considerable of interlopers, as well for her cargo vallewed at fifty thousand pounds sterling, as for the abilities of the merchants concerned, who are some of the best upon the Exchange. One Mr. Ben Reed, a school-fellow and old acquaintance of mine, formerly in the East India Company's service, and now Chief Director or Supercargo in this voyage, tould me that the persons concerned in it are not less worth than five hundred thousand pounds. And as they are able, so they are resolute to try the title of the Company. He tells me moreover, that the Lord Chief Justice Saunders hath declared to the King, that the stopping of a single ship, without shewing cause, is not justifiable by law. But whilest they are put off until the next terme, it is to be feared the voyage will be spoyled, but where the damage will light is disputeable in law.

The second ship, now lately stopt, is one Captain Blake, bound for Guinny in a ship of 300 or 400 tons. The sayles are taken off from the yardes. But in the meantyme several interlopers have gone out free this year, both to Guinny and the East Indies; I believe, more than ever went before, but they carried their designs more closely . . . . . .

Your most faithful friend,
CHRISTOPHER JEAFFRESON.

LETTER XXVI.

To the Writer's cousin, John Jeaffreson, Esq., of Rousehall, Clopton, Suffolk. Dated from London, 5 March, 168¾.

A long letter of gossip about the writer's affairs in the eastern counties. Mr. Percivall has shown himself a dishonest steward and accountant; and the writer's much-respected tenant, Mr. William Fyson, is in trouble. "What does yet more perplex me," says the writer, "is that my tenant Mr. William Fyson, with whom a new agreement was lately made for a new lease, being prosecuted as a dissenter, will hardly be in a condition to hold my farme; and, what is worse, so many of the yeomanry of that county are fallen under the same calamity, that it will be difficulte to meet with an able man for to succeed him,—in case this severity should continue, which I fear is inevitable."

LETTER XXVII.

To Captain Hill, Deputy Governor of St. Christopher's Island.

[*Note.*—Captain Richardson was the Newgate gaoler. His boldness in disregarding the directions of the Lords of the Council is an example of the official insubordination to which administrative corruption is apt to give birth. Having bought his place with a prodigious bribe, the gaoler regarded himself as having a moral right to avoid by trick and craft any orders that tended to diminish the profits and perquisites of the office.—J. C. J.]

London, 12 March, 168¾.

Sir.—The disappointment I meete with cannot be more vnwelcome to your honor than it is to me, who am only satisfied in this, that my endeavours have been no wayes wanting. But as I am obleiged to goe no faster than those, by whose guidance I move, will permit, I must be content.

I often pressed for the order, but was continually delayed; being persuaded that I might have it at any tyme, and it would be soon enough. when the men were to be had. Seeing that it must be so, I used what diligence I could; was several tymes with Captain Richardson, as if I would purchase the men of him who, I supposed, knew me not. But since I feare he did understand my businesse. For the very day that the malefactors pleaded their pardons, I went to the Old Bayley, and, tho' the Lord Mayor and Sherriffs were not gone from thence, yet Captain Richardson tould me the prisoners were disposed of. I was surprised at it; and went immediately to Mr. Blathwait, who advised me to addresse myselfe to Mr. Secretary Jenkins, which I did that night. And the next day, with a long attendance, and the assistance of Mr. Blathwait, I obtained a letter from him to Captain Richardson; which, that night, I carried to him, so soone as I had it. But he seemed little moved at it; but sayd he would wait upon Mr. Secretarie to satisfie his honor that the merchants had signed and sealed the bonds, and that, tho' the prisoners were yet in custody, the ship was ready and provision made on board for them; with such like allegations. And, accordingly, he was (as I was informed) this day with Sir

Leoline Jenkins; but how he was received,
or what effect his excuses and pretences had,
I could not learn. But without dispute, he
is left from this tyme to his own liberty.
For Mr. Secretary tould me, he would not
have you expect any malefactors until the
long vacation; and then I feare shipping
will be scarce. . . . . . .

Your honor's most obedient servant,
   CHRISTOPHER JEAFFRESON.

LETTER XXVIII.

To Ensign Edward Thorn, the Writer's agent and steward in St. Christopher's Island. Dated from London, 12 March. 168$\frac{2}{3}$.

Protesting with some severity against Mr. Thorn's neglect to write with proper frequency and fullness to his employer and friends in England. The writer is wearied with applications for intelligence respecting the young man, made by his mother and Mr. Penny. The large cargo of sugar came to a bad market, yielding only "12s 6d p. cent. cleare." In a postscript (dated 13th March) the writer says, "I pray, let Colonel Hill, your governour, know that since the writing of his and your letters, which was last night very late, I understand that the goal-birds voyage to Jamaica is stopped by vertue of Sir Leoline Jenkins, his letter, which I carryed to Captain Richardson, with whom, I think, I shall have a hearing to-morrow, or the next Councill-day, for then and there our order will be passed. But it troubles me that Mr. Blathwait will not be in town then. However, I shall do my best."

LETTER XXIX.

To Colonel Hill, Deputy-Governor of St. Christopher's
    Island.

London, 15 March, 168¾.

I writ to your honor by Captain Bowman, who went from here yesterday. But in the afternoon, the councill sitting, a petition was preferred to them, that the malefactors, last condemned to transportation might be delivered without further stopage to the petitioners, who, upon their offer to take the weomen and children with the men, had obtayned the leave of the Court, to carry them to Jamaica in a ship, that now lay ready, and had waited some tyme in expectation of those people, and had made considerable provisions of clothing and other necessaries for them. With these and the like allegations, the Councill seemed to be moved in favour of the petition more than of the order.

But so soon as I could get admittance, I stept in, and took the liberty of discourseing our whole affaire; and to show that our aime was not any ways at our private interest, but at the executing his Majesty's pleasure, signified in the order for the malefactors, for the strengthening and improving his Majesty's colony on that island of St. Christopher's, of which there was now as great occasion as ever. I urged the long tyme since this order was made, and that even till now had taken no effect. I showed how we had proceeded in prosecuting of it, and especially my last actings in it, and how Captain Richardson had opposed, and probably would oppose vs for his own advantage; the Jamaica men having a considerable profit by this way of trade; which enables them to do what we cannot afford to do, without damage to ourselves.

Thus far I went without any interruption, except some questions the Lords were pleased to put to me and Sir Leoline Jenkins. And Sir Phillip Floyd spoke something in our behalfe, insomuch that I had hopes of carrying it on our side. But then Captain Richardson was called, and one Hardies an attorney. The first was asked, whether he could dispose of his prisoners. He said "No: The Court had done it." "How shall we know that?" says the Lord President, "Where is the order?"—That could not be produced. "Will you then swear it?" says my Lord. They both said "Yes." But the Lord Hallifax was of opinion to deferre it until the next Councill Day, that all things might be brought in place. For the Lord President enquired if security were given that they should not returne in seven yeares. It was answered, "Yes;" and Mr. Hardies sayd that he was one of the securities, and could informe their Lordships of the whole matter; so Captain

Rchardson and he tooke their oaths, that it was by an order of the Court, that the malefactors were disposed of to the now petitioners.

The Attourney-Generall then fully satisfied theire lordships that the prisoners by law might be disposed of according to the pleasure of the Court; upon which and in consideration of the many weomen and children amongst the malefactors, which I could not accept, it was carried against me; and the petition was graunted.

In the meantyme, by argueing the poynt there with Captain Richardson, and alledgeing that he seeks his own advantage in the thing, I have made him my enemy more than ever. Which I matter not much for it. Their Lordships will maintaine their own order. I need not feare his opposition, for the Lord President, in the close of the businesse, tould me that for the future the Court as well as Captain Richardson would take notice of the order, and that I should be no more put by, or to that effect. For Richardson pretended he never had had knowledge

of theire Lordship's pleasure in this case,
until the prisoners were disposed of. I had
also showed the falsity of that assertion, but
Mr. Blathwait not being there was much to
our prejudice. And I found the Lord Chamberlain was Richardson's friend, and one or
two of the clerkes were active for him. I
am troubled at this disappointment, but cannot help myselfe for the present. . . . . .

Your most affectionate and humble servant,
CHRISTOPHER JEAFFRESON.

LETTER XXX.

To Captain James Phipps, a planter on St. Christopher's Island. Dated from London, 17 March, 168¾.

Announcing the capture of Bantam by the
Dutch; the intelligence of which disaster,
"togeather with the news of the loss of one
of the East India Companies ships, outward
bound, vallewed at 60 or 70 thousand pounds
has made their actions fall extremely, that is
from 230 pounds per cent to 170 pounds in
one day. It is a great misfortune to them
at this juncture." This piece of news is accompanied with a brief account of the cir-

cumstances of the victory of the Dutch over the English, and of the previous revolution in Bantam. "It is sayd," the writer continues, "the King of France offers to make a firm peace with the Germans, and to assist them against the Turks with 50 or 60,000 men, on condition they will make his son King of the Romans, which is an absolute title to the Empire, so soon as the new Emperor dies, without any further election. I expected a letter for you from our Brother Constantine; but I suppose his business has made him forget his promesse; for he is now very earnest to come to the bar, and in order thereunto has removed from Gray's Inn to the Temple; where he has done several exercises since the last term, and will the next term, I suppose, be called to the bar. Mr. Carey, Mr Kenedy, Mr. Symkins, and Mr. Wrayford and all friends are well."

LETTER XXXI.

To Ensign Edward Thorn, the Writer's agent and steward in St. Christopher's Island. Dated from London, 17 March, 1682-3.

Giving intelligence of the capture of Bantam ; and describing the great displeasure of the London merchants against the West Indian planters, because the latter do not pay their just debts to their creditors in England.

CHAPTER VI.

SPRING AND SUMMER.

(17 *April* 1683 *to* 17 *August* 1683.)

A Ludicrous Duel—Fire at Newmarket—A Gentlewoman marries a Butler—Old Books—Court Gossip—Edward Thorn's Misconduct—Health-Drinking at the Sun Tavern—The Gaoler of Newgate again—His Influence with the Council—Bribes for Placemen—Emigrants to Carolina and Pennsylvania—A Steward's cruelty to Slaves—Constantine Phipps's Fine Qualities.

LETTER XXXII.

To the Writer's Cousin, John Jeaffreson, Esq., of Roushall, Clopton, Suffolk.

London, 20 March, 1682-3.

Deare Cousen.—I am glad to hear that your eyes begin to mend, the sight being in my esteem the most pretious of the senses. Three or four dayes ago we received unwelcome news from the East Indies of the loss of Bantam, the most considerable factory the English have in those parts. The accompt we have is in short thus :—The Indian (by advice of the Dutch) took upon him the title of King in the life time of his father who it seems had too far intrusted him with the Government, to ease himself; and, being thus moved, he comes with an army and sits down before Bantam. Whiles fatherly pittie made the sire too long delay to execute his just vengeance on his rebellious son, the Dutch coming with a potent fleet to the assistance of the rebel Prince, the King was overthrown, and the English, who it is sayd stood neuters, had only time to save their goods and put them on board their ships, and so quit the factory, the Prince looking upon them as traitors. This was an unlucky accident to happen, when the credit of that company was in so declyning a state; but as misfortunes seldom come alone, so in company with this came the news of the loss of one of their ships, which had, as is reported, to the value of sixty thousand pounds in dollars, besides other goods on

board. She was cast away about the Cape de Verd Islands, where most of her men are saved. These two accidents have so far prejudiced the credit of the East India Company, that their actions in three days time fell from 230 pounds to 130 pounds or under. The news we receive from Newmarket is of a duel, in which a Linen Draper killed a vintner. The Court is not expected from thence until the last of this month. Our friends here are all well. My love to my cousen, your wife, to yourselfe and all our friends. I am, Sir,
Your most affectionate kinsman and servant,
CHRISTOPHER JEAFFRESON.

LETTER XXXIII.

To Captain James Phipps, a planter in St. Christopher's Island.

[*Note.*—The unpublished portions of this letter refer to the writer's losses in the island from the last drought, and complaints in London against the West Indian planters for not paying their just debts to creditors in England.—J. C. J.]

London, 27 March, 1623.

Deare Brother.— . . . . . . There hath happened so dreadful a fier at Newmarket, that in a few hours it consumed the better half of the town (except the Court), upon which his Majestie is returned to London sooner by five days than he intended. There hath been a report of an engagement between Captain Berry and a French frigate, which refused to strike in the English seas. Some persuade that Captain Berry is killed; others that it is a framed story. Madam Matthews is married to one Mr. Gibbs; in which match she hath only pleased herself. The man, or his concernes, I know not, but by report, which I doubt will be unwelcome news to Ensign Matthews, as I perceive it is to his brother; and I would not publish it to any but yourself, that he is a servant to Mr. Greenfield, tho' it may be of the better sort. He does (it is said) the office of a butler in that family; so that he does not live with Mrs. Matthews, who cries him up for the modestest man alive. Thus we see that we are all flesh and blood. I know Madam Hill will laugh at this news, when it comes to her eares, as in tyme it will (tho' not from me); for it is kept so private that I first heard of it at a Coffeehouse; but doubting the truth, I happened to publish part of it by my inquisitiveness.

LETTER XXXIV.

To Ensign Edward Thorn, the Writer's agent and steward in St. Christopher's Island.

London, 27 March, 1683.

. . . . . It is well you have made an end with unreasonable Mr. Rogers; but I doubt you have forgotten to demand my books that I left in his custody; the one, a Collection of the old Lawes and Orders made in the Islands in Sir Thomas Warner's tyme; the other, some Memoranda of my father's concerning the first settlement of the island; which I put no small value upon, and was very indiscreet, to part with them . . . . . I am very sorry that Mr. Van Halmaell grew so careless. I have less hopes of Doctor Hobbs, who must be strangely reformed, if fit to be trusted with the life of a human creature . . . . . The burning of Newmarket, which happened on Thursday the last, being the 22nd instant, makes well for Winchester, where his Majesty is about to build a stately palace for pleasure; and the races will be performed there until poor Newmarket be rebuilt. His Majestie came to town yesterday, having been much dissatisfied; and his game thereabouts is destroyed; and the country were very uncivil to his guards and attendants . . . . .

Your most assured faithful affectionate friend,
CHRISTOPHER JEAFFRESON.

LETTER XXXV.

To Captain James Phipps, a planter of St. Christopher's Island. Dated from London, 10 April, 1683.

An unusually long letter, consisting chiefly of trivial gossip; in which the writer speaks " of the extraordinary mildness" of the last winter, and begs his " dear brother Phipps" to give him particular information about the doings of Ensign Thorn; certain reports of whose way of life have occasioned his employer uneasiness. "I am pleased," says the writer, " that the proud ambitious humours, which seemed to lead Ensign Thorn to an itch for play and other extravagances (though with a reservednesse which, I greatly feared, only cloaked, whilst I was with him, the designs he had of acting the gallant as soon as my back was turned) have not given you any occasion of hinting some of his miscarriages. I heartily desier to know the worst of him, and I have that trust and confidence in you, that you will give me a trew information of his behaviour . . . . . I often ruminate upon the great temptations to extravagances and dishonesty that persons, intrusted with other men's estates in those islands, lay under; how difficult it is for them to live in the compass of their fortunes and condition!". . . . Ensign Thorn has had craft enough, as well as inclynations to prodigality, for to induce him to a breach of articles; but I hope his prudence will " keep him within bounds, that he will not outwit, or overact himself, but will give me occasion of rewarding rather then of complaining of his fidelity."

LETTER XXXVI.

To Ensign Thorn, the Writer's agent and steward in St. Christopher's Island. Dated from London, 16 April, 1683.

A long and not interesting letter of information and instructions, touching sales and shipments of sugar, and the management of the writer's plantations. The writer observes at the end of the epistle, " Mr. Carey, and Mr. Symkins, and Mr. Wrayford and I drank all your healths the other day at the Swan Tavern, over against the Exchange, where we meet sometymes for that purpose."

LETTER XXXVII.

To Colonel Hill, Deputy Governor of St. Christopher's Island. Dated from London, 16 May, 1683.

Announcing further impediments and difficulties in the business of the malefactors. Captain Richardson, the Newgate gaoler, has so worked on the Lords of the Council, that the writer is now required to take women and children as well as men. Moreover, the General, the Governor, Council, and Assembly of the island, must write to the Lords of the Council, for the cannon and ammunition for the fort. Mr. Blathwait further says, that the Lords of the Council should be reminded by letters of the same authorities of the wants of the island, at least twice every year. " But," adds the writer, " without *a gratification of twenty or thirty guynnies to himself,*" (*i.e.*, to Mr. Blathwait) " at the least, I doubt much the effect of the letters or anything else, which would best be done by a voluntary contrybution of some of the most able; and I should be willing to do as others. But seeing that this project of malefactors fails, I have been at several Bridewells, and intend to go again, to endeavour, by offering a gratuity to the turnkeys, to try what men I can get that way, for otherwise I find they are not to be had."

LETTER XXXVIII.

To Captain James Phipps, a planter of St. Christopher's Island. Dated from London, 16 May, 1683.

There is little news in London. "Printed papers are very partial and insignificant; and the humour of scribing is much off," so far as the gazettes and journals are concerned. "I hope," the writer continues, "that Ensign Thorn does his diligence to cleare the debts of the plantations, as fast as he can. I am endeavouring to get him some white servants, and had effected it before now, if I had not such dependence upon the malefactors, which project I have now wholly layd aside (because the women are imposed) until that poynt be cleared. Our brother Constantine and all your friends are well."

LETTER XXXIX.

To General Sir William Stapleton, Captain-General of the Leeward Islands. Dated from London, 16 May, 1683.

Relating the particulars of the writer's "endeavours towards the compassing those things you gave me in charge," *i.e.*, the petitions for recruits, malefactors, and stores, for the fort. His disappointments, in respect to the orders for malefactors and stores, the writer cautiously attributes to a *want* of something "which hath much retarded my proceedings," the something being, of course, a fund of money to distribute in presents.

LETTER XL.

To Ensign Edward Thorn, the Writer's agent and steward in St. Christopher's Island. Dated from London, 19 May, 1683.

Speaking of the difficulty of finding white servants, the writer says, "It is very difficult to procure servants, for that the English regiments in Holland raising recruits here take off abundance of the loose people; and Carolina and Pensylvania are the refuge of the sectaries, and are in such repute, that men are more easily induced to be transported thither than to the Islands." On another matter he says, "I cannot yet meet with Mr. Severine, neither at his lodgings or elsewhere, which I have endeavoured the more, for that he hath reported upon the Exchange, that my loss of negroes haith been so great, that without a supply, there will want hands to carry on the work. I rather hope it is his mistake, and that it is the bignesse of the crop rather than the death of slaves, that requires more help."

LETTER XLI.

To Ensign Edward Thorn, the Writer's agent and steward in St. Christopher's Island. Dated from London, 17 July, 1683.

A renewal of the distressing rumours, respecting a loss of slaves on the writer's plantations, causes him to write to his steward for a true statement of the case. The writer is slow to believe that Ensign Thorn has treated the new slaves harshly, or any slaves with undue severity, but requires the particulars of the mortality amongst his negroes. "You know," he says; "it is old, sturdy, and hard slaves that are to be driven to worke, and not new comers; but I was always sensible of John Steele's churlish and brutal humour, in that he was usually a companion of the old, and a tyrant over the new negroes; as if the extraordinary work gayned by over-strayning them would countervail the loss sustayned by their deaths." The writer also intimates that he hears Ensign Thorn is too often at Sandy Poynt and away from the plantations.

LETTER XLII.

To Colonel Hill, Deputy Governor of St. Christopher's Island. Dated from London, 17 July, 1683.

The Colonel's account of the cordiality, with which he has been received by the islanders, occasions lively satisfaction to the writer, who is much pleased with the Colonel's measures to raise the efficiency of the militia under his command. Colonel Worden has "promessed to speake to the Lord Dartmouth," and Captain Freeman will accompany the writer to a conference with his lordship, respecting the defences of the island, "as soone as this hurry of the plot is over."

LETTER XLIII.

To Captain James Phipps, a planter of St. Christopher's Island.

London, July, 1683.

Dear Brother.—I have just tyme to thanke you for your last brotherly kindnesse, which I received this day more to my satisfaction, than any or all my other letters, in that it brought me the welcome news of your recovery. I am not capable (if my leasure would permit me) to answer all your kind and courtly expressions, in a style suitable to them. I blush that I have no ways merrited them in the least, and for increasing your token, I absolutely disown it; for contrarywise our brother Constantine, and the rest of your relations would not permit me, so much as to pay my share of the overplus. They were all very civil to me; and without compliment, I have not an acquaintance in England that I vallew more than our brother Constantine. A man of better principles, better judgment, or better humour, I scarce know amongst all my friends. I saw him last Saturday. He was then going downe to Lee. Pardon my brevity at this tyme, and be pleased to accept the tender of my humble service to yourself and lady. I am, Sir,

Your faithful servant and loving brother,
CHRISTOPHER JEAFFRESON.

CHAPTER VII.

PLANTER AND POLITICIAN.

(17 *August*, 1683, *to September*, 1683.

A Faithless Steward.—Revoltiug Cruelty—Bad News from St. Kitt's—The Rye House Plot—Loyal Addresses to the King and Duke—Sir Charles Wheeler's Death—Duel between Colonel Nethway and Captain Billop—War declared by France against Holland and Spain—Mrs. Wiudall's Singing and Expertness on the Viol—West Indian Losses—The Writer's Mode of Life in the West Indies—Constantine Phipps at Worcester.

LETTER XLIV.

To Ensign Edward Thorn, the Writer's agent and steward in St. Christopher's Island. Dated from London, 13 September, 1683.

The latter half of this *very long* letter consists of orders and admonitions for the management of the plantations under Mr. Thorn's charge; and in the earlier half of the epistle, the writer states very clearly and strongly but temperately the many reasons he has for dissatisfaction with his steward, who had neither the courage nor the honesty to send his employer any account of the late mortality amongst his negroes, and other recent misadventures on his estate. The writer has, however, learnt the particulars of these misfortunes from several independent and reliable witnesses, who concur in the emphatic censure of Mr. Thorn's way of life. The sum of the writer's recent losses in horses and slaves, at the date of his last letters from the West Indies, was four horses and fourteen slaves, dead from cruel treatment. The losses are serious; but the writer is less affected by the importance of the injury to himself, than by abhorrence of the barbarity that has had such results. Whilst neglecting to provide sufficient and proper food and clothing for the poor negroes, the steward has overworked them, and oppressed them with execrable severities—the like of which were never known on the plantations, during the writer's residence in the island. The writer has also learnt that Mr. Thorn has become an habitual drunkard and gambler. "I often repent," he observes bitterly, "every penny that I have drawn out of England to that island, and every hour I fooled away upon it to raise an estate, for you to spend in making me ridiculous." The extravagances of the steward's abuse of his trust have made him "the discourse of the whole neighbourhood."

LETTER XLV.

To John Steele, One of the Writer's White Servants on St. Christopher's Island.

London, 12 September, 1688.

John Steele— .... I am glad to hear that your wife is arrived safe, to your comfort. I wish you all happiness and good fortune togeather. I perceive you took it ill that I did not answer your wife's request, which is very excuseable, if you knew with what difficulty at that time I got money for my own occasions; being newly arrived, and the goldsmiths most of them being at a stand, so that moneys were everywhere very scarce to be had. I confess the sum was but small, and I was ashamed to denie her so small a courtesie. I pray, remember, my love and service to her, and tell her I acknowledge myself in her debt, for the kind present which she made me from Bristoll on her way to St. Christopher's, I mean the surfet-water. I drank a cup of it in remembrance of her, since I came to London, and gave my sister and some other friends a taist of it. It was by them all judged to be very good, and indeed I thought it too good for the Tarpollions at sea, which made me preserve it so long. I am sorry you have left my plantation, and more so for the occasion of it. The losses I have sustained may partly be attributed to the unseasonable weather, and the scarcity of provisions; tho I am sensible there has beene too much neglect and misconduct on the other side. It was absolute cruelty to work the slaves by night (and new negroes too), when they wanted provisions both for back and belly. I am sure that was never practised in my tyme, nor by any considerate man that intended not to destroy his people. I perceive my affairs there call loud for me, before my businesse here will admit of my retourne, which nevertheless may be sooner than some men wish for; for I cannot indure to see myself abused, where it lays in my power to prevent it. I thank you for the account you gave me of my affairs. It was done like a friend, and so I acknowledge it to be.

Your true and faithful friend,

CHRISTOPHER JEAFFRESON.

[*Note.*—The sum which the writer had declined to lend John Steele's wife was not a trifle. She had asked for a loan of £4, equivalent to £20 at the present value of money. It was not strange that in the general dearth of money, the writer declined to advance so considerable a sum, as her husband had not asked him to do so, and her uncle was well able to supply her wants.—J. C. J.]

LETTER XLVI.

To John Holcroft, one of the Writer's White Servants on St. Christopher's Island. Dated from London, 13 September, 1683.

John Holcroft is thanked for his letter of

intelligence respecting the mismanagement of and losses on the plantations; and is strenuously exhorted to combat the despondency which disposes him to commit suicide. "I trust," says the writer, "that God will give yon more grace then, for a short term of troubles in this life, to precipitate yourself into hell. God forgive those desperate thoughts should ever any more retourne to your mind." The writer threatens, if the mismanagement of his West Indian property should be continued, to return to St. Christopher's Island sooner than "some people" may desire or think for. Still he is willing to make allowances for Ensign Thorn, who has had to contend with an exceptionally trying "season, which was enough to put a young planter out of his byasse." Should Ensign Thorn continue to maltreat John Holcroft, the latter is instructed to have recourse to Captain Phipps, or any other magistrate for protection. He is further instructed to watch Ensign Thorn closely, and report how he disposes of the produce of the plantations. "Now will be the tyme for you to observe what sugars are made, and to keep an accompt, how it is disposed of; as also of the rum and mollassus, how disposed of, and to what vallew, and to advise me of it. When sugar is making, I suppose you will be much about the worke; and, if you drive the mill, it is no shame in that country, nor hard service but what sufficient planters have done themselves."

[Ensign Thorn's tyrannical behaviour to John Holcroft was all the more offensive to the writer because he had particularly instructed the steward in a letter dated 17 July, 1683, to " be more kind to him than an ordinary servant, and let him not want necessaries for his encouragement."—J.C.J.]

LETTER XLVII.

To General Sir William Stapleton, Captain-General of the Leeward Islands. Dated from London, 13 September, 1683.

Sir William is thanked for his last gracious letter to the writer, who speaks of interviews with Lord Dartmouth and Mr. Blathwait respecting the ammunition and cannon from the Cleverly's Point fort. The letter continues, "as for the malefactors, I perceive I may have them, if I would take both sexes, which is not according to the intent of the first order. Yet I have at this tyme an inclynation to accept them on those termes, because it is probable that the Whig Plott, the discovery of which, I presume, is, by this tyme no news to your Excellency, will make the number of men, that fall under that sentence, exceed far that of the weoman; for which I expect the next sessions. My business here leyes so, that I cannot be at liberty to visit my plantation, so soone as I doubt it will want me. But I understand that your Excellency has obteyned leave of his Majesty to come for England, for a few months, which I esteem as a happiness to the Islandes, who will have one to speak in their behalfes, who best knows their wants and is the most likely to obteyne what he asks. I shall be glad to see your Excellency, and I wish your voyage may be prosperous, whenever you are pleased to take it, and that the windes and weather may be as favourable, as any that lady Russell has met with." In the following postcript to this epistle, the writer makes another reference to the Rye House Plot, which has raised his hope of soon getting a good jot of malefactors.

"*Postscript.*—My humble service to your lady; my sister Brett in like manner desires to be remembered to your lady. The islands of Barbadoes and Jamaica have made their addresses to his Majesty; and, since the horrid plot, the whole kingdom have presented theire addresses to congratulate his Majestie, and his Royal Highnesse on their delivery from the conspiracy. Sir Charles Wheeler is dead. He dyed at his house in Warwickshire, the 8th instant. Colonel Nethway called Captain Billop to account for abusive words given him upon the 'Chainge.'

LETTERS XLVIII.

To Colonel Hill, Governor of St. Christopher's Island. Dated from London, 15 September 1683.

Congratulating the Colonel on his measures for the security of the island, or rather the English interest thereof; and also on the seasonable publication and effects of "that act which, as you very well foresaw, has made no small stirre amongst the merchants." Having alluded to the hurt which war would occasion the colony, the writer continues—"I am persuaded that, whenever a war happens with France, it will be so suddaine, that there will not be any tyme to provide for defence. Therefore, it is good to be always prepared for it. The French King hath declared war with the Dutch and Spaniard, which I think is not verry acceptable to our Court; but, the Spaniards having offered affront to two of our ships, it is supposed our fleet, which was put out verry privately, will take satisfaction of them. I delivered your letter to Colonell Worthing, who promessed me, upon reading of it, to speak to the Lord Dartmouth. But I understood by my Lord that he had forgotten to speak to him. My Lord is now gone to sea with the aforementioned fleet; his departure was verry suddaine; the Duke of Grafton being discoursed of, as the person that was to go, until the fleete was almost ready to sayle. I perceive Sir William Stapleton has obteyned leave to come home for a tyme. There are instructions for every Governor, how to command the meanwhile in his respective government; and, in case of a war (as Mr. Blathwait tells me), the Governor of Nevis is to command in chief. I pray present my sister's and my service to your good lady, and tell her that Mrs. Windall and Mrs. Russell are both very well. We have been to see them both. Mrs. Windall learnes to play upon the viol, which will do very well with her sweet voice. Colonel Bayer is in Ireland. The rest of the gentlemen you mention drink your health sometymes, as we meet."

LETTER XLIX.

To Captain James Phipps, a Planter of St. Christopher's Island. Dated from London, 15 September, 1683.

A very long letter in which the writer speaks at large of his recent losses in the island, and of Ensign Edward Thorn's grievous offences. By two or three letters, dated 25 May, he has been informed of, " the death of thirteen " of his " negroes, that is, ten working slaves and three children, besides one run-a-way, and half the remaining part sick." He has heard from the same informants, that four of his horses are dead, and that the others are in a wretched condition; and that his plantation is " running horribly to ruin under the careless and evil management of a debauched, and dissolute person upon whom the whole neighbourhood complains." The injured proprietor is especially hurt by the faithless steward's shameless assertion that his cruel treatment of the slaves was a consequence of his employer's example. " John Steele," says the writer, " knows that I never worked my negroes by night, when they were not well fed by day, and that, instead of waisting my tyme at Sandy Point, or elsewhere, as I am informed Edward Thorn daily does, I was constant at allmost every meal upon the plantation, and not trusting to false, deceitful servants; with my own eyes saw the provisions distributed in order to the poor negroes, especially to those who could not shift for themselves;

which I believe with the blessing of God, saved severall of their lives in the hard tyme after the hurricanes." Glancing at the expense of time and money he has been at for the thorough settlement of his West India property, he says, "Edward Thorn's proceedings make me quite out of heart, after expending twelve hundred pounds sterling, which I really drew out of England, counting from the tyme of my going over to my coming away, which was most of it doubled there in barter or trade, and all layd upon my plantations." Still, though he cannot question the honesty of his informants, the writer is so anxious to avoid even the appearance of severity to the delinquent, that he defers to pass final judgment on him, until he shall receive his dear brother Phipp's statement of the case. Moreover, should every allegation against Edward Thorn be completely proved, his employer would even yet forgive him all his past offences, if he would change his courses and resolve to do rightly in the future. Passing from these painful matters to light gossip, the writer says, "Lieutenant Colonell Nethway haith called Captain Billop to account for calling him rascal upon the Exchainge in the hearing of several. They fought without seconds, September the eighth, at Lambeth, and were both wounded; Billop slightly in the arme, and Colonell Nethway in the ball of the sword-hand. Our brother, Mr. Constantine Phipps, is gone out of towne. The last thing he sayd to me the night before he went, was to remember him to you. He goes to Worchester, and several other parts, and will not retourne in a month."

CHAPTER VIII.

AFTER THE PLOT.

(17 September, 1683, *to* 31 *December,* 1683.*)*

Relief of Vienna—Reported Capture of Gibraltar—Lord Dartmouth's Expedition—General Stapleton's Return—Loyal Addresses touching the Rye House Plot—Exchange News and Coffee House Gossip—Court and Town—Newmarket Races—The City and its Charter—Sir Henry Tulse—The Common Council—Lord William Russell and Algernon Sidney—Aaron Smith—Sir John Knight—The Captain General of the Leeward Islands—Intrigues for his Office.

LETTER L.

To Captain James Phipps, a planter of St. Christopher's Island.

London, 25 September, 1683.

Most dear Brother. — About the 15th instant, I delivered a paquet to Mr. Baxter, which he promised to convey to you by Captain Holmes, master of a ship, that he is sending to the Leeward Islands; who is now in the Downes. My letter of that date was so tediously prolix, that, fearing to fall againe too soone into the same error, I shall now only salute you with the tender of my love, and best respects to your selfe and lady. As for news, there is little more than what I sent you in that paquett: viz., His Majestie's Declaration in a Gazette, the Lord Russell's Speech, and Mr. Lestrange's Observation upon it, and the Tryalls of the sayd Lord Russell, Captain Walcote, Hone and Rouse. The great news we have had since has beene of that blessed victory at the Reliefe of Vienna; which is the noblest and happiest action that Christendome can boast of these many years. It was a signal act of Providence, that when the besieged had, in a most gallant defence, lost more then three fourthes of their men, and were scarce able to have repulsed the enemy upon an other assault, the enemie was forced, by the King of Poland and the Emperor's forces, to march off, with the losse of 9000 men at least, 100 cannon, 50,000 tents, and much treasure. What successe they have had in the pursuit is still doubtful; but in the mean tyme all persons (except the French and the worst of the phanatiques) rejoice at this victory, and at the French intrigues of stirring up a rebellion in Poland, as well as of inviting the Turks into Christendome, being discovered. Their reputatation is so low in the esteeme of all honest men, that it may be the peace betweene vs and them will not be so lasting as some have imagined. That is, in case they should fall into Flanders (which the near approach of their armies threatens), some thinke that we should assist the Spaniard. The Prince of Orange is at this tyme at the head of 26,000 men, observing the motions of the Marshal D'Humiers, who commands a numerous and gallant army of French, and a great number of voluntiers. There was a report, some days since, that the Spaniards had yielded their strong fort of Gibralfort to the Lord of Dartmouth; but it is contradicted, being, it seemes, a mere story. But whatever the designe of the fleet is, it has beene so well carried that it is not yet known. Lord Dartmouth has thirty sayle which were fitted and dispatched on a suddaine, whilst it was generally believed that only seven or eight sayle were going for Tangier. Lieutenant-Colonell Nethway was affronted on the Exchainge by Captain Billop, soone after his arrival; upon which they had a tilt at Lambeth, with some loss of blood on both sides. The first was wounded in the hand, the second in the arme. There was nobody present but themselves, who, as I heare, behaved themselves very well. Sir William Stapelton is expected here the next Spring, having obtained leave to come home for a tyme. I hope the Island will pay Captain Jory's debt before he leaves the Islandes. I suppose the Generall will bring home the several addresses of the Islandes to compliment the King and Duke upon their delivery from the late phanatique conspiracy, which is no more than what the Islandes of Jamaica and Barbadoes have already done on other such-like occasions. Our brother Constantine is still in the country. He haith had very fine weather for his journey. I will trouble you no farther at this tyme; but with the commendations of my hearty love and service to your good lady and your selfe,

> I remaine, Sir, your ever loving brother and most faithful servant,
>
> CHRISTOPHER JEAFFRESON.

I pray, present my service to the Governor and his Lady. I writ his Honour about ten dayes since by Captain Holmes. My service to Captain Willett, Captain Pogson, Captain Crispe, Mr. Fox, and all our friends in general.

LETTER LI.

To Ensign Edward Thorn, the Writer's agent and steward in St. Christopher's Island.

London, 25 September, 1683.

Ensign Thorn.— .... This haith beene a pretty good yeare for our merchants; for what sugars they have received have sold at good rates; choice sugars at 25s. 6d. per cent. They are like to continue a commodity this yeare, for that Jamaica and Barbadoes have not fournished, nor will fournish the market this yeare as formerly they have done. Captain Bridgman, who brought the Lady Russell and Lieutenant-Colonell Nethway, is designed for Nevis againe, and will depart hence before Christmasse. It is thought that he will bring home the General, who haith leave to come home, and I hope will retourne againe; as I question not but he may if he pleases. But I am afraid the last Act for the Speedy Payment of Debts will be repealed, before he comes, or anybody be prepared to move in defence of it. For the merchants are much discontented at it, and resolve to voyd it if possible, which may be no hard matter to do when there is no opposition. The Duke and Duchess came to towne the last night. Their Majesties are expected to-day. It is sayd that the other conspirators in custody will come to theire tryalls the next weeke. Marshall D'Humiers with a powerful French army, well strengthened with volunteers, is hovering about the confines of the Spanish Netherlands; whilst the Dutch as well as the Spaniards are putting themselves into as good a posture of defence as they can to oppose the French, in whatsoever they attempt. The great defeat of the Turks before Vienna, will, it is hoped, give the German Princes leasure not only to secure theire owne, but to assist in the defence of their neighbours' territories. The Dutch have 26,000 men already in the field, and are raising more; declaring (it is sayd) their resolutions to spend all they have, rather then buckle to the French, whose designes they playnely see are to enslave them. I pray, present my service to the Governor and his lady, Captain Phipps and Captain Willett; and to Captain Pogson, Mr. Westcot, Mr. Tippet, Mr. Jessop, Mr. Sondon, and all other friends, &c., &c.

Your faithfull friend,
CHRISTOPHER JEAFFRESON.

LETTER LII.

To Ensign Edward Thorn, the Writer's agent and steward in St. Christopher's Island. Dated from London, 28 October, 1683.

Having expressed surprise at his steward's silence and apparent disinclination to keep his employer duly informed respecting the plantations, the writer repeats in temperate and strictly guarded terms the principal accusations preferred against the steward by residents in the island. Mr. Thorn is invited to give his own account of the recent mortality amongst the slaves, and the several miscarriages on the property under his control; and to clear himself, if he can, of living profusely and licentiously at a cost of £500 per annum.

LETTER LIII.

To John Steele, one of the Writer's white servants in St. Christopher's Island. Dated from London, 28 October, 1683.

Expressing regret that Mr. aud Mrs. Steele should have been treated with insult and injustice in the house of the writer, who regards the injuries done to them as wrongs done to himself, and invites his correspondent to give further information respecting Ensign Thorn's behaviour.

LETTER LIV.

To Major Crispe, a planter in St. Christopher's Island. Dated from London, 29 October, 1683.

Respecting the major's map of the island, which has been shown to Mr. Blathwait, with whom the writer had some interesting conversation, on meeting him at the Newmarket races. Should Sir William Stapleton not return to the Leeward Islands, he will probably be succeeded by Sir John Knights, who is using all his interest for that end. It will cost so much to print the map, without reducing it, that the writer hesitates to publish it. "Having," the letter continues, "entered vp his judgement against the Charter of London, his Majesty is yet gratiously pleased to permit the contynuance of the antient customes and formalities. Only he appoints the chief officers and magistrates; and several of the olde aldermen are cashiered, and new ones created to their places. This day Sir Henry Tulse was sworn Lord Mayor at Westminster, according to antient custome, with a fine appearance on the river. I suppose at land, it was as meane as last yeare, for that the Chamber of London is in a failing condition. It is this day reported that the Lord Dartmouth haith demolished Tangier, so that, seeing we cannot make it tenible, neither the Moors nor any other may make use of it. Since the death of the Lord Russell, none of the conspirators have been tryed for the late plot. It is now discoursed that they shall speedily come to their tryals; two of them, viz., Charleton and Algernon Sidney having moved for a *Habeas Corpus*, or to be tryed."

LETTER LV.

To John Holcroft, one of the Writer's white servants in St. Christopher's Island. Dated from London, 30 October, 1683.

Mr. Thorn's perseverance in insolence and harshness to John Holcroft is strongly condemned by the writer, who is astonished to hear that the steward has surrendered himself to the influence of the Irish woman who, though the writer esteemed her as fit only to be a servant of servants, is now permitted to act as though she were the mistress of his West Indian household. " A period," the writer remarks significantly, "will be put to all these disorders."

LETTER LVI.

To Captain James Phipps, a planter of St. Christopher's Island, 30 October, 1683.

After speaking at great length of Edward Thorn's delinquencies and misdeeds, and expressing his gratitude for the Captain's goodness, in visiting the plantations under the bad management of a faithless steward, the writer continues, "I hope you have received the paquet of news I sent you by Captain Helmes. Since the execution of the persons, whose tryalls I there sent you, there has not been one person tryed for the conspiracy, tho' severall are in the goales, who it is sayd will now be shortly brought to their tryalls. Aaron Smith is now in the pillory; he is fined £500 and is to finde sureties for good behaviour. It is reported that Tangier is demolished by the Lord Dartmouth, who, it is believed, went there only for that purpose, and to bring off the garrison. It was difficult as well as chargeable to maintayne it, and it is not thought fit anybody else should have it, neither Christian nor Turk. London haith lost its Charter; and its credit long before; the Chamber being in a manner shut up. But the cittie is governed as formerly by a Mayor, Sheriffs, and Aldermen. Sir Henry Tulse was yesterday sworne as Mayor. Sir John Knights, of Bristoll, is discoursed of as the person most likely to succeed Sir William Stapleton, in case he should not retourne again to those parts, as it is commonlie believed he will not. I heard it reported that his Majestie had promessed it to him; and that the Lord Halifax had wished him joy. I know Captain Freeman is his great friend; and I am apt to believe (as I may hint to you) that if he carries it, nothing but a plentiful harvest will secure the planter from the merchants, who will have a good friend in him. But I shall have tyme and opportunities to informe you more of this matter, before it take effect. Our brother, Mr. Constantine Phipps, is well. We drunke your health togeather but two nights since, when he toulde me he would write to you. I sent you a letter by Colonell Warner's son (dated the 25th of September) who went with Captain Jonathan Frances, &c., &c.

I remain, Sir,
Your obedient servant, and affectionate loving brother,
CHRISTOPHER JEAFFRESON.

LETTER LVII.

To Captain James Phipps, a planter of St. Christopher's Island. Dated from London, 26 December, 1683.

In reply to an account of Ensign Thorn's behaviour by the captain, who appears to have taken a lenient view of the steward's errors and indiscretions. Though he declares his extreme pleasure at the tenour of this report, the writer confesses his indisposition to dismiss his suspicions of Mr. Thorn, and enumerates in a very long epistle all the grounds he has for thinking ill of the young man.

LETTER LVIII.

To Ensign Thorn, the Writer's agent and Steward on St. Christopher's Island. Dated from London, 26 December, 1683.

After remarking that Mr. Thorn has exhibited no account of the profits and losses of the writer's plantations, in accordance with his agreement, nor done anything to relieve himself of discredit in his employer's regard, the writer announces that he has sent out two white servants, a man named John Benninfield, bound for two years, and a woman, named Katherine Bull, bound for five years. Particulars are given of articles provided by the writer for their outfit.

CHAPTER IX.

HARD WINTER AND COLD SPRING.

(January, February, March, 1683-4.)

Colonel Gamiell's Death—Sir Edward Brett's last Illness and Death—Small Pox in London—Turkey Tottering— European Politics—Negociations with Mr. Blathwait— Lady Russell's West Indian Friends—Apprehensions of War between England and France—Sir Nathaniel Johnson—The Spanish-Dutch Combination—Rye House Prosecutions—Captain Richardson's Extortions—The Thames Frozen Over—Frost Fair—A Fatal Season— Hardships at Sea—William of Orange—Governor Hill's Influence—Mr. Sedgewick—The First Client.

LETTER LIX.

To Captain James Phipps, a planter of St. Christopher's Island.

[In this letter attention is again called to Mr. Blathwait's appetite for gratuities, and the necessity for gratifying it. Sir Edward Brett, whose death is mentioned in the epistle, was one of the writer's connections by his sister's marriage with Charles Brett. In October, 1665, Sir Edward supplied John Evelyn *(vide* "The Diary") with "some horse to bring up the rear" of the five hundred Dutch prisoners, who were marched from Maidstone to Leeds Castle. Sir Edward is entered in the first edition of "The Present State of England," as Serjeant Porter of the King's Household, with two yeomen and four grooms under his command.—J. C. J.]

London, 12 February, 168⅔.

Dear Brother.—Since the 20th December, the use of the pen has beene a most unpleasant exercise. The season haith been so severe, the like was never felt in the memory of man. Its effects have been more sensibly felt in Flanders, France and Holland; where, in several townes, they could not keep open their shops, men were frosen to death in the streets, some of the horse-soldiers dropt down dead from their horses, with many such sad consequences, of which, praysed be God! we have had few examples in England. But here likewise the condition of many thousands was very deplorable; but great collections were made for the releif of the poor, by his Majestie's especial command. All trade was at a stand; and the small-pox has reigned in most parts of England, but both raged strangely in London. The very Court has had its share. So that the mourning dress is now the fashion here, and is suitable to most persons' present condition as well as mine, who have lately buried my father-in-law, Colonell Gamiell, and am now about to lose another very good friend, Sir Edward Brett, who is past all hopes of recovery.

Few aged persons have beene able to resist the hard season. I bless God, I endured it very well, and have yet escaped the small-pox; which is a great blessing for one so lately come from the West Indies. Several persons seeme to threaten vs with a contagion, which some have so far believed, as to report the plague to be broken out already amongst vs. But (God be thanked; who will, I hope, preserve vs from the heavy judgments), I see not the least signes of it hitherto. . . . . Our brother Constantine is well; and *virilem togam sumere* will be his businesse the next terme, when he expects a lawfull call to the barre; where I hope he will stand my friend, for I shall be proud of such a friend, into whose hands I can with so much confidence commit my interests in the businesse, which he is now entering upon.

The news at present is more forraine then domestick. The Gazet gives a large account of the victory and preparations against the Turk, whose empire begins now to shake. To come nearer home, our expectations are great what the event of affairs will be. It is much douted, we shall not be able to continue onr neutrality. The French king is reported to be low in his treasure, as he is in the hearts of his people. It is reported that he has offered a truce for twenty yeares, but it is like to be refused. His neighbours desire to be no more abused by his treaties. It is thought great endeavours will be used to engage vs in the warre; the Spaniard,

Dutch, and several of the Electors of Germany seeming to threaten the prosecuting of Monsieur as the common disturber of the peace of Christendome; and my comfort is that, if we be forced to a breach with him, his hands will be so full, that the West Indies will scarce deserve his care; insomuch that I find the treaty, that Captain Crispe came home about, might safely be concluded, Almost any thing the English will ask in reason, I was told that Mr. Blathwait could get done; *but I seemed to slight it, for that I know the gratification is wanting which he must have in hand, before he moves in any of those affairs.* Mr. Plott haith solde his moyety of Colonell Morton's plantation to Mr. Baxter. The third of January, the Lady Russell gave a general and very splendid entertainment to her West India acquaintance. I perceive she hopes Sir James will succeed Sir William Stapleton. I cannot tell what to think of it. Sir John Knights waits diligently at Court; and whether Mr. Plott aims at it or no, I am not certaine. People's opinions are divided in these matters:

and all that I can say is that, if Mr. Plott has such a designe, he manages the best and most privately. Sir Edward Brett's death interrupts me. I have tyme and opportunity to inform you what I heare by other ships, that will be going a month or two hence. I feare a warre with France will be inevitable, tho' we are not inclined, or prepared for it. I hope you are in a better posture in the Island of St. Christopher's. We are full of divisions and factions, which should make vs pray for peace with our neighbours, as well as at home. I pray God send you your health, and protect you and prosper you, which are the continuall prayers of him who, with the commendations of all love and service to yourselfe and your lady, remaynes as ever,

Your faithful humble servant and most affectionate brother,

CHRISTOPHER JEAFFRESON.

Postscript.—Sir Nathaniell Johnson is the person that will succeed Sir William Stapleton.

LETTER LX.

To Colonel Hill, Governor of St. Christopher's Island.

[The writer again insists on the necessity of bribing the Secretary for Foreign Plantations into a disposition to do his duty to St. Christopher's Island.—J. C. J.]

London, 12 February, 168¾.

Honoured Sir.—. . . . . It is no small satisfaction to all others, as well as myselfe, who are any ways concerned in the Island of St. Christopher's, to hear of the care your Honour has taken about the fort and fortifycations of the island, which are very considerable, considering the apprehensions that many people have at this tyme of a warre with France, which may happen, considering the eagerness of the Spaniard and Dutch to draw their neighbours to a league offensive and defensive against France. . . . . What has happened since I writ Captain Phipps his letter, makes me think there will be no parliament this year; for the Lord Danby was this day admitted to bayle, and likewise all the Lords in the Tower, who

were committed upon the Popish Plot . . . . .
I will speak to Mr. Baxter to haisten the powder your Honour haith writ for, being willing to forward all things that may tend to the putting of the island in a posture of defence; and I am very free to give my consent, that the guns, your Honour mentions, may be mounted on my Plantation; desiring only that something may be entered in the Secretary's office, to prevent the conjectures, that some persons may hereafter draw from thence, that part of my plantation is King's land, which in tyme might alter the property, at least of all that lies below the common path. Otherwise, I shall thinke much to employ any part of my plantation to the service of my King and country, and I must acknowledge myselfe extreamly obliged to your Honour, that you would so kindly advise me of the designe before it was put in execution.

I am glad that Mr. Blathwait is likely to receive a present from the island. It may make him willing, who, we know, is in the way of doing more service to those parts then another can; and I have fear that he has been disobliged by the want of it. For he haith not given me such incouragements to wait on him, as might induce me to hope for an advantage by giving him those troubles. He tould me plainely, that I must take the women as well as the men, if I will have any of the malefactors; which has made me to expect your Honour's pleasure, which by a former letter I requested you would signify to me, if we should take them upon those terms; which were to destroy the designes of his Majestie's order, for the strengthening the colony, at present. Not but that women might work, and in tyme help to people the island. The last Gaol Delivery, Mr. Panden, Mr. Cary, Mr. Symkins, &c., thought to have the malefactors. But Captain Richardson was too hard for them, though they had given fifty shillings for every prisoner. Which it seems was too little, tho' for us it had beene too much, seeing we must pay five pounds *per* head passage; which they would not do by I suppose at least one halfe, by reason they would victual the ship themselves, so that a passage would not stand them in above three pounds at most. However, the act that they shall serve nine yeares will be a great incouragement. . . . .

* * * * *

This is the first day that the streame has appeared to move in the Thames, since it was frozen over. It was about the beginning of January, that people first walked over it. The various divertisements and passetymes upon the ice, with the many booths, coaches, and chariots, togeather with Frost Faire (as it was called) drew great crowds of all sorts, sexes and ages of people upon the ice; where it was better walking than in the streets, and better for the coaches, that plyed from the Temple to Westminster bridge for sixpence. But as these novelties pleased the mobils and kept such in warme exercise, who wanted both fire and employment, so that thousands of poor soules suffered great hardships; and in France and Flanders the cold was so intollerable, that people fell down dead in the streets.

Neverthelesse what has happened between Christians and infidels does equal almost the proceedings of a summer campaigne, as the Gazet will show at large. But the preparations of the Venetians to assist the Emperor, and the supplyes the Pope is sending to him, give great hopes that the next summer will be fatal to the Turkes, especially if, as some say, the Persians come into the league. This day, Sir Edward Brett payd that debt which we all owe to Nature. I believe the bitter season haistened his end. The inclosed I designed to send before the frost, as you may perceive by the date of it.

Your Honour's most obedient servant,

CHRISTOPHER JEAFFRESON.

Postscript.—Mr. Hambden was this day fined fourty thousand pounds for high misdemeanour.

LETTER LXI.

To Ensign Thorn, the Writer's agent and steward in St. Christopher's Island. Dated from London, 12 February, 168$\frac{3}{4}$.

Announcing the equipment and shipment of two servants, a man and a woman, for the writer's plantation.

LETTER LXII.

To Captain James Phipps, a planter of St. Christopher's Island. Dated from London, 15 February, 168¾.

A hasty acknowledgment of the receipt of letters. The writer says in a Postscript, " I have sent you another Gazett, which is well worth your reading; the trial of Algernon Sydney, Esq., ; and the print, which describes the various pastimes and sports on the River of Thames, as were really performed during the late hard frost."

LETTER LXIII.

To Ensign Thorn, the Writer's agent and steward in St. Christopher's Island. Dated from London, 11 March 168¾.

In answer to the Ensign's ineffectual attempt to clear himself of the serious charges brought against him by eye witnesses of his profuseness, cruelty, licentiousness, and flagrant disregard of his employer's interest. The writer shows himself by no means satisfied with the steward's lame and tardy defence, tho' he still seems willing to forgive the offender, who is enjoined to prove himself worthy of credit by behaving honestly in the future.

LETTER LXIV.

To Captain James Phipps, a planter of St. Christopher's Island. Dated from London, 12 March, 168¾.

A long answer to a letter in which the Captain endeavoured to palliate Ensign Thorn's misdemeanours, and to demonstrate that they had been greatly exaggerated. The writer insists that he has been guilty neither of injustice nor excessive harshness in his letters to the steward, who, when charity has done her utmost to cover his sins, is seen to have been guilty of gross outrages on morality and decency. The employer seems willing, however, to let bye-gones be bye-gones, provided Ensign Thorn will behave properly in the coming time:—" I hope the effect of his dilligence for the future may make amends for what is past." Sir Tymothy Tyrrell, Lady Russell, and all Sir James Russell's friends are equally surprised and mortified by the appointment of Sir Nathaniel Johnson to the office of Captain-

General of the Leeward Islands,—a post which Sir Timothy had made sure of for his son, which Lady Russell expected would fall to her husband, and which Sir John Knights of Bristol had been "pushing for" with equal zeal and openness. The Spanish ambassadors are pressing the King of England to furnish eight thousand men towards the protection of Flanders, in accordance with the stipulations of the treaty of Wimmingen; but the King and his Minister take another view of their obligations.

LETTER LXV.

To Major Crispe, a planter of St. Christopher's Island.

London, 11 March, 168¾.

Worthy Sir. . . . . My sister Brett presents her service to yourself and lady. Colonell Gamiell has taken his last leave of the world. He was near sixty-nine years of age, but hearty and lusty, till his violent pains of the stone, which he most complained of, took him off his legs. He was ill about a quarter of a year, and dyed about the begining of January; since which event Sir Edward Brett is also dead.

But this winter haith made many mourners; the extreme sharp weather, though it came at the most seasonable time of the year, being more severely cold than haith been known in the memory of man. Several persons were not able to indure it. Especially the aged and sickly were swept away; so that the bills of mortality increased two hundred a week. The small-pox raigned very much at the same time. In the meantyme, the youth, that could not worke, drove away as well as possible the cold, and their sufferings, by various sports and passtymes upon the River of Thames; whilst thousands, who could not be so frolicksome, underwent such wants and miseries as can hardly be imagined, although the charity of the people (according to the royal request and example of his Majestie) was more liberal than the ordinary; collections being made in the churches as upon a briefe.

The ships, that lay beating upon the coast, and could not abord any shore for six or eight weekes suffered greater hardships (being deprived of the meanes of relief). Several perished, and amongst the rest a rich East India ship, which was at her setting out fallen upon by several Indian vessels, from whom with very much courage, and no less difficulty they freed themselves; and coming home, after having taken some men out of a Virginia vessel, which was in a perishing condition, they themselves were reduced to a pound of bisquet per weeke a man; and being by that means almost famished and extremely weak, they were cast away in the Channel, and few if any of the men saved.

Great preparations are being made almost all over Christendome, for the approaching summer's warre; but that which concernes us most, is the French designe upon Flanders, which the Spaniards are not able to defend, nor the English or Dutch ready or willing to protect. The Prince of Orange is the only person, who vigorously opposes the French ascendancy to that degree, that he is by no means to be persuaded or wrought off from opposing the greatness of France; and who is of so warlike and daring a spirit, that in history he may hereafter rival Lewis in the tytle of great, if he be not too soone cropt from the field of honour. The Amsterdamers are factious, and the Prince's enemies frighten the people with apprehensions, that he aimes at raising an army to establish himself in that government; which has succeeded, by the French underhand assistance, to do him much prejudice amongst the people, who will not agree to the raising of sixteen thousand men, with which they are obleiged to assist the Spaniard in Flanders.

The fleet that went with the Lord Dartmouth is not returned from Tangier. The bad weather scattered them in the Mediterranean Sea, and did some damage to them. But there was none but some small victuallers lost.

Sir Nathaniel Johnson (formerly one of the farmers of the Hearth Money) is preparing for his voyage to the Leeward Islands, where he hopes to succeed the present General in his Government; but he will not (as I am informed) imbarque before Sir

William Stapleton arrives here; so that they may conferre about the affaires of those parts to which Sir Nathaniel is a strainger; as we are all to him. But he bears a good character &c., &c.,

CHRISTOPHER JEAFFRESON.

LETTER LXVI.

To Colonel Hill, Governor of St. Christopher's Island. Dated from London, 10 March, 168¾.

Acknowledging the gratifying terms in which the Governor, Council and Assembly to St. Christopher's Island, have expressed their sense of the value of his services to the island. The guns and ammunition have not yet been sent to St. Christopher's from England, in accordance with the instructions of the Council for that purpose, because Lord Dartmouth's departure for Tangier has stayed the execution of such orders. Sir. William Stapleton is returning to Europe, of his own free will, and with the frendliest feelings to his appointed successor, " who is a very loyal person, and has rendered his Majestie such acceptable services, that it is reported the

King sayd, that he long wanted an opportunity of rewarding him." "I wish heartily," the writer continues, " that Mr. Blathwait may receive his present from our Island by that tyme Sir William arrives, or before, that he may be inclyned, and incouraged to assist me in what I shall endeavour in behalfe of St. Christopher's, which must be done before the new Generall goes out, or not at all." The Governor is reminded that he would do well to ask the Earl of Feversham to induce both the King and the Duke of York to speak a word in his favour to the new Captain-General; although there are no grounds for supposing Sir William Stapleton's retirement will be prejudicial to Colonel Hill.

LETTER LXVII.

To Captain Phipps, a planter of St. Christopher's Island. Dated from London. 12 March, 168¾.

Touching the character of a gentleman who would be a suitable successor to Mr. Thorn, on the writer's plantation, should the Ensign wish to retire from that property. Though he avows his intention to employ

Mr. Thorn for another term, should he wish to be retained, the writer is obviously arranging to rid himself of the froward young man, who does not condescend to write to his master oftener than once in three months, and has an insuperable aversion to book-keeping. The gentleman (Mr. Sedgewick), who eventually succeeds Ensign Thorn in the stewardship, is described as one who " has traded to Virginia and Barbadoes, and is a gentleman born." The writer adds, " I knew him when his mother kept her coach, but misfortune has so attended on him, that I should be willing to put him in a way of living." The letter has the following postscript; " my sister presents her service to your lady and self, whose healths she drunk yesterday; our brother Constantine and I doing the like. He is to be my counsell the next terme, and is in effect the same now. We are going into the couutry together at Easter about a law business of mine, which has long depended."

LETTER LXVIII.

To Captain James Phipps, a Planter of St. Christopher's Island. Dated from London, 24 March, 168¾.

Touching Ensign Thorn's refusal to submit his accounts, for the writer's plantations, to the inspection of Captain Phipps and Captain Willett, in accordance with the articles of agreement between himself and his employer. Copies of those accounts have, at length, been sent to the writer, who deems them very unsatisfactory. " I have with this," says the writer, "inclosed my letter to E. Thorn, which, if you take the trouble to peruse before you send to him, it will informe you what passes between us. By clapping a little wax under my seal, you may prevent his knowledge of its being sent open. . . . . . The next weeke I am going out of towne with our brother Constantine, and shall be out neare a moneth; for our journey is long, which may, I feare, hinder my writeing to you so so soone as otherwise I might do."

CHAPTER X.

THE HOT SEASON OF SIXTEEN-EIGHT-FOUR.

(June, July, August, and September, 1684.)

The Duke of York—A Military Demonstration—Sir Thomas Jenner—The Writer appointed Political Agent for St. Chistopher's Island—He presents a Congratulatory Address to the King and the Duke of York—Old Silver and New Plate—Extortions at Newgate—The Rogues' March from the Old Bailey to the River—Arms for the Malefactors—The Recorder's Triumph and the Gaoler's Victory—Three Partners in a curious Venture—Mrs. Lewis of Glamorganshire.

LETTER LXIX.

To Captain James Phipps, a planter of St. Christopher's Island. Dated from London, 30 June, 1684.

Having given a summary of the latest news in European politics, written in the style of the public news-letters of the period, the writer observes, "On Thursday last, the

Duke of York headed the artillerymen, and, as he marched in great state on a managed horse, in a courteous but princely manner saluted the people, who were numerous, and whose huzzas and acclamations bespoke him the darling of the people. I have now obteyned another Order of Council, that no men-malefactors shall be transported to any other colony, but that of St. Christopher's, untill the 300 men be sent. But Sir Thomas Jenner, and those who are like to be sufferers by it, are resolved to oppose me in it. When I brought the Order to him, he seemed very uneasy at it, and made several objections, saying he must discourse the King in it. But I hope it will worke some good effects; as it ought, for within this moneth this Order hath cost me neare eighteen pounds. Mr. Cary is married to one Mrs. Right, a Turkey merchant's daughter, and haith a good fortune with her. Some say near £2,000."

LETTER LXX.

To Colonel Hill, Governor of St. Christopher's Island.
Dated from London, 30 June, 1684.

Containing intelligence respecting the new Order in Council for the transportation of three hundred malefactors to the island. The epistle contains also a sketch of the present state of European affairs.

LETTER LXXI.

To General Sir William Stapleton, Captain-General of the Leeward Islands. Dated from London, 1 July, 1684.

Touching the new Order in Council for the transportation of malefactors to St. Christopher's Island. "The reason," the letter states, "why the first Order was ineffectual was that the profit accrewing to severall officers upon the transportation of malefactors is so considerable, that they will not willingly forego such advantages." With regard to Sir William's purpose of placing his sons at Westminster school, the writer remarks, " Mr. Blackburn shewed me a letter of your Excellency's, wherein I was mentioned, as one of the persons he was to advise with about removeing the young gentlemen, your sons, from Camberwell to Westminster Schoole; but I understand the Lady Marsh is too tender of them to part with them to such harsh masters, as the masters of that schoole are reputed to be."

LETTER LXXII.

To Colonel Hill, Governor of St. Christopher's Island. Dated from London, 25 August, 1684.

Reporting further opposition to the writer's endeavour to obtain malefactors, with no women, children, or infirm persons amongst them, and without payment of the usual exorbitant fees to the gaoler of Newgate and the Recorder of London. Sir Thomas Jenner, the Recorder, flatly and steadily refused to obey the mandate of the recent Order in Council, regarding the matter, and produced in his justification an order under the King's sign manual, directing malefactors to be taken indifferently, without any kind of picking and choosing. After several interviews between the writer and such civic authorities as Sir Peter Daniells, the High

Sheriff, and Sir Thomas Jenner, the Recorder of London, the writer, yielding reluctantly to his adversaries, consents to take the malefactors, without regard to sex, or age, or bodily vigour, and to pay both the prison-fees and Mr. Recorder's fees.

LETTER LXXIII.

To Colonel Thomas Hill, Governor, and to the gentlemen of General Sir William Stapleton's Council, of St. Christopher's Island. Dated from London, 25 August, 1684.

The Governor and Council of the island having elected and authorised the writer to present their addresses to his Majesty and the Duke of York, on their preservation from the late conspiracy, and also to act as their London " agent for that island," the writer announces that he has already presented the addresses, and (with suitable expressions of regret that no gentleman, of greater influence at Court, and large knowledge of affairs can be found for the office), he promises to do his best for their interests, as their duly appointed and accredited Political Agent. Thanking the Governor and Council for their present of £50, the writer declares his intention to use it only for the good of the island; as he desires no reward for his service to St. Christopher's Island, except the satisfaction of promoting its welfare.

LETTER LXXIV.

To Captain James Phipps, a planter of St. Christopher's Island. Dated from London, 25 August, 1684.

Having stated in what way he has dealt with the watchmaker and goldsmith, who has undertaken to repair the Captain's watch and articles of silver, the writer passes to the consideration of European politics. *Apropos* of the chances of a rupture between England and France, the writer says of the treaty of neutrality, for securing perpetual amity between the French and English colonies on that island, "as for the Treaty of Neutrality, you know I was never fond of it; and I am less so than ever, seeing the perfidiousness of that people is so apparent in this age, that their treaties of peace are but stratagems of war."

LETTER LXXV.

To Ensign Thorn, the Writer's agent and Steward in St. Christopher's Island. Dated from London, 5 December, 1684.

Concerning the business of the plantation, and the shipment of the first lot of malefactors; the venture of importing them into the colony being undertaken at the joint and equal pecuniary risk of Governor Hill, Mr. Vickers, and the writer.

LETTER LXXVI.

To Captain Pogson, a planter on St. Christopher's Island. Dated from London, 3 September, 1684.

Respecting minor matters of insular politics. Prescribing for his friend's distemper a herbal preparation, that was in good repute amongst sufferers from the gout in the seventeenth century, the writer says, " I am heartily sorry to heare that you are so tormented with your olde distemper. I will presume to tell you a small remedy, which worked miracles on a friend of mine. It is only this:—Take radish-leaves and fry them in sallet oyle, so that they be dry and crispe; and then apply them."

LETTER LXXVII.

To Major Crispe, a planter on St. Christopher's Island. Dated from London, 4 September, 1684.

Speaking of the terms, at which he has taken the first lot of malefactors, the writer says, "I hope in a few days to put some of the malefactors on board Captain Size. I met with greater letts and difficulties than ever could be imagined. But, when I consider that the sheriffs, Mr. Recorder, and Captain Richardson are the opposers, and also the losers by the bargain, I wonder not at it. For, though the payment of all the prison fees, and charge of conveying them safely on board ship be cast upon us, who are concerned (the Lords of the Treasury passing over the Order without giving any directions in it), yet it will not amount to above four or five and forty shillings per head, whereas others used to pay four or five and fifty shillings. Being tired out with the clamours against me, and the uneasiness of the persons I had to deal with, I was content to comply for this time, rather than suffer some inconvenience, and have a contest with those great men, who owe me enough ill will already."

LETTER LXXVIII.

To Colonel Hill, Governor of St. Christopher's Island.

London, 8 September, 1684.

..... Captain Size has undertaken to deliver to your Honour, or your order, the malefactors named in the list, which I herewith send you, with an account of their trades, according to the best information I could get. The charges upon them are greater then I expected. I esteem the arms we send with them to be almost as necessary for the island as the men. It is my desire that when the servants are disposed of, it may be for ready goods, and that no division of goods may be made; but that what sugars and other goods are collected, or received, may be shipped, and returned home upon a joint account; so that the full product may be divided amongst us concerned, which will be an assurance as well as an encouragement to us to be concerned for the next parcell, which I hope will come with much less difficulty, when we have found out the method of doing it, which has cost me an intollerable deal of trouble.

And now at last, Captain Richardson designing to deliver the malefactors at the prison doors, we are in a perplexity how to secure them on board; for we have reason to doubt some foul play, if it be possible to put it upon us. I have been labouring all this morning to obtain three files of musquetiers, and am denyed them; because the soldiers, as the officers say, must not intermeddle with the civil power, unless upon a very special occasion (as that on the Lord Craven, his order; the Court being now at Winchester.) Nor are soldiers permitted to go one mile out of town. So that, Captain Richardson denying us his men, I am forced to look out for volunteers, that is who ever we can get to assist us. The security we have given is five hundred pounds, to transport the malefactors to the island of St. Christopher's; and upon the delivery of them, I suppose Captain Size will request a certificate under the hands of your Honour, that so many malefactors were landed and delivered on shore on the island; without which our bond will not be delivered up, in which Mr. Baxter, Mr. Vickers, Captain Size and his mate, and myself are bound by order under the King's signe-manual.

We have beene forced to take two or three infirme men, but they have trades. The bursen man is a shoemaker; the lame man is a glover; but at the worst, it may be expected that the other lusty fellowes, especially such as have good trades, will make amends for the refuse. For we are under no obligation to dispose of the tradesmen at two thousand pounds of sugar per head, which, considering they are to serve eight years, is we hope the least they will fetch—without their armes, which may be vallewed at 400 pound a man; which is very cheape for sword, belt, cartouche-box and gun (all good serviceable armes). But your Honour is concerned for an equall share with us; and we must refer ourselves wholly to your Honour, whose good directions and management of the affairs we wholly rely. . . . . .

Your Honor's most obedient and faithfull servant,

CHRISTOPHER JEAFFRESON.

A List of the convicts, ordered to be delivered, and which are to be transported to the Island of St. Christopher by Captain Size.

Men.

1. James Griffith, a shoemaker.
2. Jacob Watkins, a seamen.
3. William Flack, a sawyer.
4. John Cary, a clerk.
5. John Barnet, a labourer.
6. John Codd, a grocer.
7. John Francis, a butcher.
8. John Smith, a weaver.
9. John Voller, a vintner.
10. Richard Enos, a glass-maker.
11. Robert Voller, a glover.
12. Richard Ford, a shoemaker.
13. Roger Wickley, a husbandman.
14. Stephen Bompstead.
15. Robert Whealy.
16. Charles Atlee, a boy.

17. Nathaniel Sunderland, clerk.
18. Christopher Ashley, a ship's carpenter.
19. John Howard, a hatt-presser.
20. Gerard Midleton, a vintner.
21. James Harden, a hatter.
22. John Wheeler, a taylor.
23. William Fletcher, a haberdasher; he is well-bred, and has good friends.

Women.

1. Ellenor Adam.
2. Margarett Paule.
3. Joan Nichols.
4. Mary Dusoe.
5. Alice Cronfield.

In all 28 malefactors.

LETTER LXXIX.

To Colonel Hill, Deputy-Governor of St. Christopher's Island. Dated from London, 11 September, 1684.

Touching the terms paid for the malefactors. In consideration of the resoluteness of those who oppose the Order for shipping malefactors to the island, and the inconveniences they occasion, the writer thinks that after all it would be best for him to pay the full fees of 55s. per head on the convicts to the Recorder and gaoler; "Mr. Recorder having twice declared that this business of the transportation of the convicts in this manner is £30 or £40 out of his way; which, if so, will be a considerable loss in the 300."

LETTER LXXX.

To Captain James Phipps, a planter of St. Christopher's Island. Dated from London, 13 September, 1684.

Respecting malefactors transported by Captain Size. At the close of the epistle, the writer says, "Our brother Constantine Phipps has been out of towne these three weeks, at Mr. Jackson's, at Lee, but he has made two or three trips to towne. We had appointed to be merry together with Mr. Vickers at the fayer, but the raines prevented us. It is not a week since I saw him. He was then very well, and designed to write to you. The Court is at Winchester, and we have no news."

LETTER LXXXI.

To Ensign Thorn, the Writer's agent and steward on St. Christopher's Island. Dated from London, 13 September, 1684.

The Ensign is instructed to exert himself to dispose of the malefactors at good prices, and also to collect and get in the sugar and other commodities for which they may be sold. "The Governor," says the writer, "Mr. Vickers and I are concerned; which you must keepe to yourselfe, for it maybe his Honor would not care to have it known; tho' I am sensible Mr. Baxter" (Governor Hill's London agent) "will make no secret of it." Having dealt with matters of business, the writer continues, "My sister was married two dayes since to one Mr. Lewis, a gentleman of good estate and good family.* He has a very good character amongst all his neighbours in the country. They will spend the winter in towne, and the summer in the country. I see no likelihood, but that it will be as happy a match as has been made

---

* Mr. Lewis's estate lay in Glamorganshire.—J.C.J.

this many a day; their humours and dispositions agreeing extraordinary well, as I have observed in the tyme that I have been acquainted with him, which was some tyme before I thought of being related to him. The nuptials have made me idle these two or three days."

CHAPTER XI.

DOMESTIC AND PUBLIC AFFAIRS.

(17 September, 1684 to 29 October 1684.)

Edward Thorn's Misconduct—Constantine Phipps's Marriage—Sir Robert Sawyer, the Attorney-General—Lord-Keeper North—Sir Francis Withins—Chief Justice Jeffreys—Charles the Second and the Prince of Orange—Mr. Chidly—Van Bewmingen—The Bantam Claims—Siege of Buda—Lord Mayor Sir William Smith—Court Gossip—Religion and Loyalty in Fashion—Dejection of the Whigs—Imprisonment of Titus Oates.

LETTER LXXXII.

To Ensign Thorn, the Writer's agent and steward in St. Christopher's Island. Dated from London, 13 October, 1684.

Discussing at great length questions that relate to the steward's mismanagement of the plantations. That the epistle is not devoid of complaints may be seen from this passage :—

"When I heard of the death of one of my servants, I supposed it must be John Holcroft; which your letter confirms. I am indeed heartily sorry for that loss; for I looked upon him as a sober, honest young man, and, though not so serviceable as was expected, he might have been more so, when seasoned to the country. But, if he did not want for anything and was well used, I am the better satisfied; which I do rather believe, because you never had any reason, that I know of, but to be kind to him. I hear you have lost another of my horses. It is strange ill fortune that they have found a way of breaking their necks, one after another of late. But I would be careful not to make my letter unpleasant to you, did not the complaints of the poor tenants sound harshly in my ears. *That,* tho' you pass it over in silence, I cannot. It is the most unwelcome news that I have heard this many a day. I perceived they cryed out before the mill was finished that their canes were spoyled, which in one of my letters I did touch upon; but if from the time you began to grind to the latter end of August you have not satisfied them, I have great reason to fear we shall come by damages; which, indeed, I shall be very uneasie at, as I am also at the injustice, which is done to the poor people, which may justly draw a curse upon us; which God avert, together with those stormes, which would give them occasion to charge us as the means of all their losses."

LETTER LXXXIII.
To Captain James Phipps, Planter of St. Christopher's Island.

[In the connections which Sir Constantine Phipps formed by his early marriage appears *one* of the explanations of his professional success. Before the date of this letter, Sir Francis Withens had so far lived down the discredit of his expulsion from the House of Commons in 1680, that he could be named as a powerful and eligible patron for a young barrister.—Chief Justice Jeffries was in the brightest hour of his brief triumph.—In the 'Life of Lord Keeper Guilford,' Roger North gives a kindly sketch of his cousin, Sir Robert Sawyer, whose success is attributed to the Lord Keeper's countenance of a meritorious relative. The 'State Trials' afford conclusive evidence that Sir Robert did his utmost to bring his niece's husband into notoriety and employment. Having held a brief for the prosecution in the trial of the Rev. Thomas Rosewell, the non-conforming minister, at the King's Bench for High Treason in October, 1684, Constantine Phipps opened the case for the Crown, in the following year, against Charles Bateman, John Feneley, William Ring, Elizabeth Gaunt, and ex-Sheriff Henry Cornish, on their several trials for High Treason. He was also retained as junior counsel for the Crown in the two prosecutions, in May 1685, of Titus Oates for perjury. Once also, during the same year, he was retained in a State-Trial as advocate for a victim of politico-religious persecution. When the pious and venerable Richard Baxter, clerk, was tried before Lord Chief Justice Jeffreys, for publishing a seditious libel, five counsel were retained for his defence, viz. Messrs. Wallop, Rotheram, Atwood, Williams and Constantine Phipps. The three first-named counsel having only irritated the judge, and injured their client by their excellent arguments, the two last-named barristers deemed it best to be silent. "Mr. Williams and Mr. Phipps said nothing, for" it is recorded "they saw it was to no purpose."—J. C. J.]

London, 24 October, 1684.

Dear Brother.— . . . . . The other watch, according to your order, I delivered to our brother Constantine Phipps, who upon Sunday last was a seven night entered into sacred bonds of matrimony, to his own and all his friends satisfaction. He was not long about it; but has made a very prudent choice. I have not seen the young lady, for I was to go out of town the very next day after they were married, nor can I informe you of particulars. For her own fortune, she had a thousand or five hundred pounds, I dont know which. But our brother told me, that the Attourney-Generall adds one thousand pounds more to it. He gave the wedding dinner, and is extraordinarily kind to his niece and his new nephew; and this kindness of Sir Robert Sawyer is to be esteemed a fortune of itself; for he, being Attourney-General, will not only countenance our brother and bring him into practice, but has also already recommended him to his cousen, Lord Keeper North, and to Sir Francis Withins, one of the judges, who have both promised him all kindness and assistance imaginable. He will be introduced to the Lord Chief Justice Geoffreys, and several others. Which helps being given to a man, qualified as he is in every respect of natural as well as acquired parts, it can hardly fail but that he will be a rising man. God giving a blessing to his endeavours, and granting him long life and health (for which I shall ever pray), I question not but he will rise to great honours. And places of dignity best become such as he is; whose good example of piety, loyalty, temperance and sobriety will more powerfully influence those in a lower grade, than when they moved in the same sphere with him. Indeed, it would be much for the good of Church and State, if there were more of such as he, especially in places of trust and dignity. Let me not seem a flatterer, because I say these truths to a brother. It is out of the abundance of my heart that I utter things well known to all his friends and acquaintance. 1 can assure you, I rejoyce in his good fortune; and being his clyent I have some reason to hope the better of my cause. It is now term tyme, which, with the amours at home with the young lady his bride, may prevent his writing to you by this ship, tho' he told me he designed it, when I sayd I would advise you of your new sister. All your friends are well, except Mr. Jackson. Mrs. Reeves has been ill. The Counsellor, notwithstanding his late nuptials, is every day at Westminster Hall, where we meet, and sometymes go out to drink your health, as becomes brethren.

Be pleased to read the enclosed, to seal it, and send it where directed. I have writ some little news to Colonel Hill, which I know he will impart to you. It is all I then had. But since the close of the letter, there is a report of the misunderstanding between our King and the Prince of Orange. It came to that degree, that all correspondence between the Prince and Mr. Chidly, the English resdent in Holland, is forbidden by both parties. The Prince and Van Bewmingen are sayd to be reconciled, and to make one interest, by which means the —, who is very rich, is also made very powerful. It is likewise reported the Commissioners are coming to treat upon the demands made by us of £1,300,000 for the injuries done us at Bantam in the East Indies. I wish all differences may be amicably concluded; but I assure you it is much doubted of. I think the English have as much reason to court peace now as ever they had. I desire you to be private in discoursing these affaires; for they are yet carried privately. All the discourse of the town is Buda, which, if famine does not force it to surrender, will I fear hold out longer than the season, that will admit the Christians to keep the trenches or maintain the siege, which has cost us dear. Sir William Smith is Lord Mayor for this year; and on Wednesday last, he made a splendid show, according to the Citie Custom,

> Your faithful humble servant, and loveing Brother,
> CHRISTOPHER JEAFFRESON.

LETTER LXXXIV.

To Major Joseph Crispe, a planter of St. Christopher's Island. Dated from London, 27 October, 1684.

A long letter, in which mention is made of the writer's repeated attempts to bring about a reconciliation between the Mayor and his brother in England, and of the shortcomings of Ensign Thorn. Of the unprofitableness of the plantations, in which he has sunk so much capital, the writer says, " I am sorry we soon lose the hopes you had given us of seeing you in England the next summer. It is a pity you have not set some bounds to your designs in the improvement of your plantation. I heartily wish that, whensoever you think fit to leave it, it may answer your expectations better than mine has done,—I mean, proportionately to the great expenses you have been at, and the tyme and industry that you have spent upon it. I find that a small estate in England is more valueable than a great one in the Indies, where one does not design to live; for I send supplies thither, whence I expect return, tho' I have received none to the value of one barril of sugar since, I left the island. And if such a plentiful year, after eight or nine years' labours and expenses for improvements, will not produce one hogshead of sugar clear, there is small incouragement for me to supply the wants of able slaves."

Towards the close of this long letter, the writer says, "His Majesty came to town the other day from Newmarket. I shall endeavour to get Mr. Blathwait to show him your draft, that it may be printed, which has been my desire ever since it was sent over; and the reason, why it is delayed or obstructed, is a riddle to me. The Duchess of Portsmouth came the last week very ill from Newmarket, and some say she will hardly recover. All things else seem in a way of recovery. Atheism and disloyalty grow out of fashion. The Church and State begin to flourish more than ever. The Whigs hang their heads. Oates is a prisoner, almost past all likelyhood of releasement, unless it be with a pass into the other world, which some expect. Another Nonconformist preacher was the other day arraigned, and will be tried this term for speaking treason in his sermon, which may cost him his life. And a merchant will be tried for returning moneys to Sir Thomas Armstrong after he was outlawed."

CHAPTER XII.

NEWS FOR THE PLANTERS.

(29 October 1684, *to* 6 *December* 1684.*)*

A Review on Putney Heath—Goodman the Player—Rosewell the Preacher—A Duel in a Play-House—Great Fire in the Temple—A great Fire at Powys House—Van Bewmingen and the Duke of Monmouth—The Bantam Claims —The Earl of Rochester—The Siege of Buda—Recent Appointments—A Talk of the Town—Official Changes— The Scotch Parliament—The Duke of York.

LETTER LXXXV.

To Colonel Hill, Governor of St. Christopher's Island.

[*Note.*—The omitted passages of this letter relate to the malefactors already transported, and to the writer's interview with Sir Thomas Jenner, the Recorder of London, respecting the shipment of another lot of convicts—J. C. J.]

London, 29 October, 1684.

Honoured Sir—. . . . . . I am infinitely obliged to your Honour for the kindness you did me, in appeasing the complaints of my tenants, whose case is very sad and deplorable, not beyond my pity though without the reach of my help. But, with your Honour's leave, I have this to plead in my excuse, that the death of my horses and cattle, by which means my cattle-mill was rendered useless, has freed me from the. . . . . or at least the penalty of breaking their canes in tyme.

The first of this instant was a rendez-vous on Putney Heath of four regiments of foot, and all the Horse Guards and Grenadiers, and the Earl of Oxford's regiment. But the day was so wet that his Majesty stayed but a short time on the heath. Last Saturday was seven-night, the Duchess of Portsmouth came from Newmarket sick, and continues dangerously ill. His Majesty came to town on Thursday last. Yesterday Mr. Goodman, the player, was indicted for hiring a doctor to poyson the Duke of Grafton, the Duke of Northumberland, and the Lord Peterborough, with some other persons of quality. Which the said doctor proved under his hand, but Goodman denyed it, and offered such bayle as was not accepted. So he was returned to Newgate He was very fine, and talked boldly; but the Lord Chief Justice was sharp upon him, and told him he must not huff the Court. It is reported that the D— of Cleveland keeps him.

This next day, one Rosewell, a Non-conformist preacher was arraigned for a treasonable sermon of his. Sir James Hackett, lieutenant-colonell to the Lord Dunbarton's regiment, was wounded in the thigh by one Mr. Potter in the playhouse; of which wound he has since died. He is much lamented by his Majesty, and all that knew him.

On Saturday, last there happened a fyre in Fig-tree Court in the Inner Temple. It was put out without much damage, except where it began, and the very same night a great fyre broke out in the Lord Powyses house, occasioned, as is said, by a pan of charcoal set in his closet, to drie it, for the house was but newly finished. It was burned to the ground; and many rich jewels, much plate and money, and noble furniture, with a rare collection of pictures, were destroyed. The whole loss is computed at thirty or forty thousand pounds, for his share. The damage done to the neighbouring houses, was small in comparison. . . . . .

Your Honour's most obedient servant,
CHRISTOPHER JEAFFRESON.

LETTER LXXXVI.

To Captain James Phipps, a planter of St. Christopher's Island. Dated from London, 10 November, 1684.

A long letter in which the writer sets forth the way in which he has, in his dear brother's behalf, executed certain commissions; how he has caused watches to be repaired; has sold old and bought new silver plate; has purchased a periwig and some trifling articles of jewellery.

"In your tanckard," says the writer, "I have exceeded what you seemed to desire in the weight; but I esteem it the worst husbandry to make such a piece of plate slight, when it is to containe such a weight as two quarts will be. It is substantial, and with good usage may last many years; and, whenever it comes to be changed, it will fetch what it cost, all but 6*d.* per ounce for the fashion, and 2*s.* 6*d.* for the coat of arms its ingraving. I saw your old silver weighed, and stood by, whilst it was cut all into little pieces, and put into the crucible, and melted down. Then, immediately carrying it back to the goldsmiths, I saw it weighed again, and found the loss of melting, much less than I expected; it not being neare half an ounce. They did so undervalue the plate on accompt of some coarse that was amongst it; and the trying of it at the Hall was the only meanes to know the real value of it, which was 4*s.* 3*d.* per ounce, which comes to £8 1*s.* 6*d.*, as appears by the goldsmith's note, a copy whereof I have herewith sent you. The perriwig, which is in the tanckard, was made by one, Sedgewick, (whose brother, the chyrurgion, I have seen at your house). He makes my perriwigs, and does protest this to be an extraordinary good one, and makes me believe I have a great pennyworth in it at 3*l*. and 5*s*. He made it on purpose for you, and desires to have the custome, (he says) of you and your friends, as this proves in the wearing. But keep it as dry as you can; for rain is a great enemie to perriwigs."

Closing the long narrative of these pieces of small business, the writer continues, "In my last letter I gave you to understand that Counsellor Phipps was married to Sir Robert Sawier's, the Attorney-Generall's niece, and the Lord Keeper's cousin, a good fortune with good friends, which makes all his acquaintances adore him as a rising sun. I gave you also an account of a misunderstanding between the Dutch and us. The matter is this, the Prince of Orange being reconciled to the great statesman Van Bewmingen (who has been looked upon as a creature of the French) shews great countenance to the Duke of Monmouth, who lives publicly in a great house in Amsterdam, which gives great distaste to our Court. The Dutch are sending over Commissioners to treat about the demands of 13—100—1000 pounds for the damages done to us at Bantam in the East Indies. I see no ground, or probability, for the reports some men create, as if there were a likelyhood that the French would joyne with the Dutch against us the next Spring. If there be anything that looks like it, I will advise you of it by the first opportunity. I wish for peace with all nations, at least, till we are better united amongst ourselves. It is said that the Earl of Rochester is going Lord Lieutenant of Ireland; which was much opposed by the Lord Arron (the Duke of Ormond's son) but to no purpose."

LETTER LXXXVII.

To Colonel Hill, Governor of St. Christopher's Island.
Dated from London, 11 November 1684.

There have been violent storms at sea. Twenty ships belonging to London merchants, have been lost; three of them perishing between West Chester and Ireland, "in one of which were thirty thousand guinneys." A stout strait's ship called the " Leopard" has been wrecked off Lundy Island. But the alarms of those storms have no effect on the Governor's daughter, Mrs. Windall, who holds to her purpose of making the passage to St. Christopher's Island, and has consented to bear the present letter to her father. Mrs. Lewis being at her husband's place in Glamorganshire, the writer has for a time given up his lodging in Channell Row, and begs that his letters may be addressed to him at the house of Mr. Poyntz, upholsterer of the sign of 'the Goat' in Cornhill. The Lords of the Committee of Trade, after hearing Mr. Story of the Temple in behalt of the merchants, have refused to pass the two Acts, sent over from Nevis and Mountserrat. As for the Act from St. Christopher's Island, the writer is urging Mr. Blathwait to get their Lordships to read it. The Christians have been forced to raise the siege of Buda; and the world is wondering how the Duke of Lorraine will contrive to bring off his army. "The good agreements," the writer continues, "that there are between the Prince of Orange and Van Bewmingen, and the kind entertainement that the Duke of Monmouth receives at Amsterdam, make us jealous of the Dutch, and angry with them. I heare that the Commissioners are now coming over to treat upon the demands made of £1,300,000 for the injuries done us at Bantam in the East Indies. Some fear a war, but I hope better. The Earl of Rochester is going over Lord Lieutenant of Ireland, in the Duke of Ormond's place. It is reported that the Lord Hallifax shall be Lord Treasurer, and the Lord Godolphin, Lord Privy Seal, Colonel Kirke, who commanded-in-chief in Tangier, is sayd to be going over Governor of New England. The jury at the Guildhall gave £10,000 damages against Mr. Papillion for arresting Sir William Prichard, when he was Lord Mayor. The Dutchess of Portsmouth is recovered of her illness. The Lord Garrett of Brumly," (*i e.* Gerard of Gerard's Bromley) "dyed suddainely in a taverne, not above a month since, and was burried last week. The revenue of the four and half per cents is put into the hands of Commissioners, of whom Mr. Henry Carpenter is nominated for one; the other is an Irishman, and goes over from hence. I understand that Mr. Blathwait designs to substitute one under him in the Islands."

LETTER LXXXVIII.

To Ensign Edward Thorn, the Writer's agent and steward on St. Christopher's Island. Dated from London, 11 November, 1684.

In reply to an epistle in which the Ensign has endeavoured to persuade his employer that the unproductiveness of plantations (which were abundantly productive whilst the owner was upon them) is altogether attributable to accidents and the faults of inferior servants, for which he cannot be held accountable. The writer stigmatizes Mr. Thorn's statements as "fond pretenses and vain shamming excuses," which only render their utterer ridiculous. "Can you," the dissatisfied employer asks in regard to one of the excuses, " think it the part of a prudent or carefull steward to suffer his two years' labour to be almost lost by a few workman's negligence."

LETTER LXXXIX.

To Colonel Hill, Governor of St. Christopher's Island. Dated from London, 6 December, 1684.

Announcing that in consequence of his petition, preferred last summer, to the Lords Commissioners of the Treasury for the Order from the King and Council, the writer has been summoned once and again before their Lordships, who in the end returned him the Order, with the endorsement of, "Not to be done" on it. The writer has ascertained that their Lordships' reason for this course was the absence of any danger of a war with France, whereas "when the first order for the three hundred malefactors was made in 1677, there were great apprehensions of a warre with the French." The agent for St. Christopher's Island has thereby learnt that the Lords of the Treasury will not help his colony, unless moved to do so by the alarm of an instant danger. It is remarked that their decision in this matter does not spare the King's purse; as the four or five hundred pounds, to be paid by the colony in additional fees, will all "goe into private persons' purses."

Mr. Blathwait informs the writer that the Lord Keeper is framing an "Act for the Islands in General, for the speedy and just payment of debts, instead of the repealed Act" for the same purpose. The writer continues, "Sir Thomas Lincke, the Governor of Jamaica is dead, and Sir Phillip Howard has that command, and is preparing for his voyage, the Duke of Northumberland being to commande the Queen's troop of Guards here. Colonell Kirke is to go Governor to New England this Spring, and a draft is to be made of the King's Guards, for a detachment of foot to be sent with him. It is sayd that the Duke of York will goe for Scotland in March to the parliament to be held there in the Spring. There have been many discourses, which are commonly believed that the Duke of Monmouth was in towne but last Monday. Letters from Flanders to severall merchants say that he was set upon by six highwaymen, and that he killed two, and the rest fled for it. On the

14th of the last month, Mr. St. John and
Colonell Webb, with severall Wiltshire gentlemen, being in company at the Globe
Taverne in Fleete Street, a quarrell happening, one Sir William Estcourt was unhandsomely murdered, as is supposed, by the
aforesayd persons, who are in Newgate.
The town talkes lowdly of the barbarous
circumstances of this and severall other base
murders, lately committed. Dr. Ken is
made Bishop of Bath and Wells, in the
roome of Dr. Meux, who is translated to the
Bishopric of Winchester, on the death of
Dr. Morley."

LETTER XC.

To Ensign Edward Thorn, the Writer's agent and steward
on St. Christopher's Island. Dated from London,
8 December, 1684.

Complaining that the steward persists in
withholding his accounts from Captain Phipps
and Captain Willett, to whom he is bound,
by the articles of his agreement with his employer, to submit them once a year. Further
it is remarked how the steward seems bent
on keeping his master in the dark respecting

the same accounts; the statements of receipts and expenditure for the previous year being mere "shamming shadows of accounts." God has blessed the Leeward Islands with an abundant year; but the writer knows not whether he will profit by the abundance.

LETTER XCI.

To Captain James Phipps, a planter of St. Christopher's Island. Dated 6 December, 1684

Accompanying "a book compiled of all the works of the author of 'the Whole Duty of Man,'" which the writer begs his friend to accept; and containing a tedious recital of Ensign Thorn's offences. Dealing with a more agreeable subject, the writer says, "The Counsellor (*i.e.* Constantine Phipps), "grows a great practitioner, and is like to be eminent. I expect to see him in print before Christmass, when Rosewell, the Nonconformist Parson's 'trial' comes forth (who is convicted of High Treason). Con : Phipps, Esq[re], who opened the matter, must fill the first pages of the booke with his pleadings. And likewise in the tryall of Mr. Hayes, he bore a part; but the prisoner was acquitted, haveing a favourable jury. .... My sister Lewis gives her service to yourself and lady. We went together one day this week to wait on our sister Phipps, and to wish her joy, hoping to have found our brother at home, the terme being over. Tho' we missed of him, we met with a pretty obleiging young lady. She is a comely handsome person, well bred, courtly and ingenuous, and in every respect so well accomplished, that I hugely applaud our brother's choice of a young lady, who seemes to promesse all the happinesse that a man can propose to himselfe in a good wife." The writer adds, "Sir Phillip Howard is to resign his command of the Queenes troop of Horse Guards to the Duke of Northumberland, and to go Governor of Jamacia, in the room of Sir Thomas Lincke, who is lately dead there. Some twenty or thirty desperate Scotchmen have broken into open rebellion, and have killed two or three souldiers, and committed several outrages, to purchase their own destruction. I am told there will be a parliament there this Spring, and the Duke of York will be there as High Commissioner of the Kingdom.—Sir Nathaniell Johnson makes preparations, as if he designed still for the Generalship ; but I am persuaded he will not go till our Generall comes over, and not then, if Sir William Stapleton desires to retourne. Captain Billop would fain goe over with Sir N. Johnson, and presses him to a speedy departure.

LETTER XCII.

To Sir William Stapleton, Bart., Captain-General of the Leeward Islands.

London, 6 December, 1684.

Sir.—As I have given your Excellencie an account hitherto how I have proceeded upon the order for the 300 malefactors, I presume to continue giving your Excellencie that trouble. Since Captain Size (who carried away 26 convicts, men and women) sailed out of the Downs, a petition, which I preferred to the Lords Commissioners of the Treasury, was read. It had layne before them several months, and was intended to procure a second reading of his Majestie's Order in Councill, which had beene layd aside without the effects we expected from it. Upon my petition I was ordered to attend; which I did many dayes before I was admitted, and then, after several questions asked me, I was ordered to attend again next day; when it appears Sir Peter Dashwood the late Sheriff of London was also ordered to appeare. I was not then called. But upon hearing him, their Lordships sent out his Majestie's Order again, with these words indorsed upon it—'*Not to be done.*' By which I am debarred of any hope or expectations to have the prison-fees discharged by the Sheriff, as was proposed. But I designe to proceede to take off the next parcel of convicts, as we did the last; hoping that the Island, as it is it's interest, will see the adventures complied with, and their returns made so that we may not be loosers. Before I concerned myself, I proposed it to severall merchants, traders to the Island, who generally declyned it, and tould me that a man would not see his own money again. But, having gone so farre in the businesse, I was resolved to venture farther, and not let it fall in that manner; and I do not see how we can be any great loosers by it,—tho' probably the profits will be inconsiderable, counting the many hazards we run.

The 10 of March, the Parliament opens in Scotland, where the Duke of York will be then present in person. Sir Phillip Howard is preparing to go Governor of Jamaica, Sir Thomas Lincke being dead since July last; and the Duke of Northumberland is to commande the Queenes troop of Horse Guards in this place.

Colonell Kirk, late Governor of Tangier, is ordered to go to New England, as Governour. But he is to carry no souldiers with him, as was at first discoursed.

The Lord Lansdowne is going Embassador to Spain. Mr. Soames is going Embassador to Constantinople, the Lord Shandois being called home. Several other embassadors are being despatched to Denmark, Sweden, &c.; several affaires of great consequence, whether for warre or peace, being to be negotiated in Christendom this winter, as is believed. It is whispered that the Lord Sunderland is likely to be made Lord High Treasurer of England.

I shall give your Excellency no further trouble for the present, only adding my prayers for your health and prosperity, and for the happy voyage of Your Excellency, and your Lady and family, when you imbarque for England. &c., &c.,

 Your Excellency's most faithful, and obedient servant,

  CHRISTOPHER JEAFFRESON.

CHAPTER XIII.

THE CROWN PASSES.

(January and February, 1684-5.)

Rumours about Monmouth—Murder of Sir William Estcourt—Episcopal Changes—Constantine Phipps at the Bar—Official Appointments—Ambassadors to Foreign Powers—Resistance to the Turk—Rumours of War—Arrest of Colonel Danvers—Ministerial Honours—Scotch Convicts for the West Indies—Charges against Patrick Trant—Illness and Death of Charles the Second—James the Second's Accession—A quick Voyage from the West Indies—Charles the Second's Funeral—Restoration of the White Staff Officers,

LETTER XCIII.

To Captain James Phipps, a planter of St. Christopher's Island. Dated from London, 17 January, 1684-5.

Touching the price of sugars and freight; and referring to Ensign Thorn's neglect to exhibit his accounts. "The French troops," the writer adds, towards the end of his mercantile epistle, " are drawing towards Italy, threatening Genoa with a siege, so soone as the season will permit; which is likely to engage the Spaniards as well as the Italians in the defence of it; whilest all Germany will have enough to do to stop the torrent of the Turkish armies, which will be poured in upon them this summer in prodigious numbers, for which they have been preparing all the last year."

LETTER XCIV.

To Colonel Hill, Deputy-Governor of St. Christopher's Island.

London, 17 January, 168$\frac{4}{5}$.

Sir.—Since my last letter to your Honor, I was called by Mr. Blathwait's appointment to attend upon the Lords Commissioners for Trade; where Sir Thomas Jenner, appeared at the same tyme, when instead of that favour which I expected from their Lordships, in pursuance of their order, and in lieu of the prison fees which the Lords of the Treasury do not see fit to discharge, the Lord Keeper (who, I conceive, had been

misinformed in the business), represented
me to the rest of the Lords, as a person
who, moved by a private interest, desired
to take my choice of the malefactors, and to
sell them to the merchants; which impu-
tation, howsoever erroneously suggested
against me, I found very difficult to remove.
Whilest Sir T. Jenner (from whose interest
I have reason to believe this proceeds)
urged the great inconveniency of separating
the men from the women. At last, the Lord
Keeper sayd that (if the rest of the Lords
were of his opinion; who by silence
seemed to assent) Mr. Recorder should use
me kindly, and give me the refusal, and
then, if 1 would not take them indifferently
one with another, then he might dispose of
them as formerly.

It would be tedious to relate my objections, or the arguments on both sides; which
were made to theire Lordships, till they tould
us that we might withdraw. I was much
surprised at this unexpected reception and
slight put upon their Order, and the dis-
couragements from my supposed friend, Mr.

Blathwait, who tould me that Sir T. Jenner espoused it as his own interest, which I know is greater then myne. But, nevertheless (since Mr. Vickers came to towne) we have been with Mr. Recorder, to let him know our resolutions to take the malefactors off as formerly. He says he knew of no free pardon yet, and that there would be as many women as men. I sayd it was so much the worse for us; but howsoever for this tyme we would take them, till we could remove the hardships, which are now imposed upon us, as I hope we may when oure Generall arrives here as is expected this Spring.

There is little news stirring, but a rumour of a probability of a war with the Dutch, in order to which some thinke we shall have a Parliament this spring, after that in Scotland is over. Severall very scandalous libels have lately been dispersed, relating to the death of the Earl of Essex, and divers persons have been taken into coustody, others being sought for, and more particularly Colonell Danvers, who has writt some, and dispersed others. A hundred pounds is offered to anyone that shall take him. It is discoursed that the Lord Keeper will be made an Earl, and Lord Chancellor, and the Lord Chief Justice a Viscount, and the Lord Rochester (who is preparing to go for Ireland as Lord Lieutenant) a Marquis. The Duke goes for Scotland next moneth.

The weather is extreame cold, which spoils writing, and haistens me to conclude with the tender of my most humble service to your Honour and your Lady, and to Mrs. Windall, togeather with the like from &c., &c.

CHRISTOPHER JEAFFRESON.

LETTER XCV.

To Colonel Hill, Deputy Governor of St. Christopher's Island.

[In the first half of this epistle the writer deals with a matter, arising out of the malicious endeavour of some of his enemies to sow dissensions between him and his correspondent. Of course, the sad news of the Gazette was the intelligence of the the death of Charles the Second.—J. C. J.]

London, 19 February, 168¾.

Honoured Sir.— . . . . . There are now 400 or 500 men in Scotland, who are offered to be delivered, all or part, on board any shippe, which shall be sent to Edenboro' for them; security being first given there that they shall not escape, but be transported to St. Christopher's. But, having proposed it (as I was ordered) to most of the considerable merchants trading to the Leeward Caribbe Islands, I do not find any of them willing, or inclinable, to meddle with them, except Mr. Vickers, who likewise is not resolved.

There was discourse that Sir Nathaniell Johnson was promised a shippe by the Duke to transport him very speedily. I desired my friends, who belong to the Duke, to be inquisitive, and to let me know if it were so, and I spoke to Sir Thomas Dupper of it, and went together with Mr. Vickers to the Earl of Feversham and to Colonell Worden, who promised, whenever there was occasion, to procure the King's order for your establishment. But now I do not see any likelihood that he should go before Sir William Stapleton comes, if then. I am told he is a proprietor of Carolina.

Mr. Patrick Trant has been accused of some injustice in his accompts, upon which he was put out of the commission, and likewise Mr. Bridges.

The French have given great distrust to the Court of England by an order published in France, directing the maritime officers there to seize and bring into their harbour at Toulon all English vessels bound to Genoa, to unlade them, and paying their freight to let them go, intimating that it was done with the consent of the King. Several of our ships were accordingly seized, and carried to Toulon; but I think Monsieur is made sensible of his error, and hath released the shipps with their cargoes, and by a civil letter he hath, as I am tould, declared that he desires to preserve and maintain the union between the two countries, which I hope will be continued. But this gave occasion to the generality of people here (who are always more desirous of warre with

France than we that are concerned in the Leeward Islands have reason to be) to talk loudly of warre; especially since this our great chainge. But for that sad news, I had rather the enclosed Gazette than my pen should declare it. I thank your Honour for your letter by Captain Brecknell, and the newes, which was very acceptable to hear, that St. Thomas is like to be no more a harbour for pyrates. Sir, be pleased to give myne and my sister's humble service to your lady and Mrs. Windall, and be pleased to accept the same from him, who, *maugre* all the aspersions of misguided pens, shall remain &c., &c.

Your Honour's most faithful and obedient servant,

CHRISTOPHER JEAFFRESON.

LETTER XCVI.

To Captain James Phipps, a planter of St. Christopher's Island.

[The long opening paragraph of this letter refers to the Captain's purpose of coming to England in the same ship with

Sir William Stapleton. In case he holds to that purpose, the Captain is urged to provide himself with clothing and other means to enable him to endure the cold of the Northern seas. For the same end, he is enjoined to select a good, weather-tight cabin. He is reminded that he is entitled to the best cabin in the ship, after the one taken by His Excellency.—J. C. J.]

London, 19 February, 168$\frac{4}{5}$.

Dear Brother. . . . . You will find us, when you come, all in deep mourning, which is the dress I have been most acquainted with, since I came over. This is for a great and common loss, in which we are almost all equal sharers, and which I suppose will be no news to you, when you read this. Otherwise, it might surprise you as much as it did us. On Candlemas day in the morning, the King, being suddenly seized with a fit of apoplexy, was for near two hours in our apprehensions dead. But being revived, he lingered out a short and painful remainder of life, till the Fryday morning following, and then about eleven of the clock he yielded to nature, and left the throne to his brother, who was proclaimed King James the Second that same afternoon : and may his raign continue and end as peaceably as it has begun ! For tho' all people were astonished and grieved at our great and suddain losse; yet none seemed in the least dissatisfied at the righfull succession of oure now Gracious Soveraigne, who has given such assurances of the security of our religion and properties, that all fears and jealousies being removed, we hope for a happy and flourishing Government. Which God grant!

Sir, I have herewith sent you the case you writ for : this being the first shippe, that has been dispatched from hence, since the arrival of Captain Phippard, who had a quick passage, and was fortunate in that the former letter miscarried; by which he is excused from the payment of the Insurance, which I should otherwise have made on him by your order. But not having your farther directions, I have not insured on Journall, hoping that there is no occasion for it. I hope your case will prove good and every way to your content. I bought it of Mr. Hunt, whom I esteemed the best, if not the cheapest casemaker in London.

Ensign Thorn sent me over ten hogsheads of very ordinary sugar, in Captain Phippard; and seven on Mr. Avery's accompt. I thanke you for demanding his accompt, which I expected, and he promised long since. It is strange, it should not now be ready, as it should have been made up at midsummer: but I must expect no better from him. I referre you for farther news to the Gazets, which I have sent and which are very full. I shall not inlarge because I know not whether this will find you at St. Christopher's, for which reason I have sent the Gazets to Captain Willett, as well as the Governor, at either of whose places you may see them, if you are upon the island when they arrive. Our brother Constantine Phipps is well. His lady haith had the small-pox, and was in some danger, but is now recovered. I pray give mine and my sister's service to your good lady, and be pleased to accept the same yourself from,

Your most faithfull humble servant and loving brother,

CHRISTOPHER JEAFFRESON.

LETTER XCVII.

To Ensign Thorn. the Writer's agent and steward in St. Christopher's Island.

[The omitted passages of this epistle relate to freights and prices of sugar and other West Indian products, and to the work of the plantations J. C. J.]

London, 19 February, 168⅘.

Ensign Thorn—. . . . . I received yours by Captain Phippard, with the hogsheads of sugar, which, though it be a small quantity in comparison of what I expected, and tho' the sugar be bad, and the freight dear, yet it is very welcome, and I thanke you for it; but it does not come to so good a market as you supposed. I fear it will not clear me above eight shillings the hundred. When Mr. Wrayford saw it, he sayd seventeen or eighteen shillings the hundred was as much as it would yield. . . . . . I will not renew the advice, which has been so much scorned and derided, knowing it would be as much in vaine as ever it has been. But I desire you would ship me more sugars as fast as you can; not being injurious to my creditors. For I have a very chargeable law-suit now in hand, with defendants in six or seven several counties, and in those counties with many and powerful adversaries. My only comfort is that I am plaintiff: but it keeps me bare of moneys, and makes a present of ten or twelve hogsheads of sugar, or less, very acceptable to sweeten a term.

If it be not the first, it is the most earnest request that ever I made you, that you would make me some considerable retournes, answerable to your promise and my expectations. If ever you designe to oblige me, let it be now, that it is in your power. For I suppose you are now very busy in grinding; this being usually the best time of the yeare for it. You were kinde in advising me of the Governor's displeasure, which is without cause on my side. For I don't see we have more reason to be troubled that we are so much concerned in it than otherways; and as for procuring the men by means of his friends, it is so great a mistake to suppose that I ever spoke to any of them of any business whatsoever, in which I myself was the least concerned. But I know who has done me that ill office. The Governor will know his friends from his flatterers, when he has tryed them longer.

In retourne of the news you sent me, I can write you such bad news as is usually so swift of flight, that before this comes to your hands, it will probably so far have lost the quality of news, that it will be only a memento, to renew your sorrows, for the great loss of our most Gracious King, who has been suddainly snatch't from his unworthy people. I saw his Majestie on Sunday night, the first of February, as well as ever to my thinking; and the next morning, the first news I heard was that he was dead; but he came to himself again, and after languishing four days, on Friday morning he chainged his earthly crown (as we hope) for a better. For he made good use of that short time; the bishops often praying beside him, and his expressions being very good. King James has given gracious assurances to the people, that the Church of England shall be preserved and protected. But the Gazetts, which you will see, will inform you of all proceedings more largely than my letter can do. I have sent one to the Governor, and one to Captain Willett, where you can see the proclamations and declaration to the Council. Let not my negroes want necessary provisions. Neglect of negroes is the ruin of a plantation.

Your friend,
CHRISTOPHER JEAFFRESON.

LETTER XCVIII.

To Captain Willett, a planter on St. Christopher's Island.

London, 19 February, 168¾.

By Captain Phippard I received ten hogsheads of sugar from my plantation, which is the first fruits I have received from thence, and I am sensible that, as I cannot reap those advantages without the great trouble of such good friends as yourself have appeared to be, so my thankes and acknowledgements are most due to you; and whilst with blushes I pay those unprofitable debts, I have hope of opportunity and meanes to expresse my gratitude in some better manner, which, if you will not direct me on, I must endeavour to find out, if it be possible. For I am really ashamed to be so very burdensome, and troublesome to you, as my business has become, and is like to be so long as you continue such kindness to me; who find so great necessity for trespassing upon your good will, and for accepting those offices of friendship, which you are pleased to render me, that I must aske for a continuance of those favours, and that in a particular manner, in the absence of Captain Phipps, who is, I understand, coming off for England.

I have sent enclosed a Gazett, which will be the messenger of sad news to you; if you have not before its arrival heard of the death of our King, who was privately interred in a vault in King Henry the Seventh's chappell at Westminster on the 14th instant. The solemnities were much the same as at any pompous funeral; and most of the nobility in towne were assistant at it. King James has restored most or all of the White Staff officers to their places again. It is sayd that we shall have a parliament in May, and I hope all things will be happily settled to the satisfaction, as well as the peace of the Kingdom; which God grant,

Sir, Your most faithful humble servant,
CHRISTOPHER JEAFFRESON.

CHAPTER XIV.

THE NEW REIGN.

(2 March 1684-5 to April 1685.)

Loyal Adresses to the New King—Edward Thorn's Dismissal—Transient Coldness between the Writer and Governor Hill—Another French Fleet—Sickness of the Horse Guards—Preparations for the Coronation and Opening of Parliament—The new Steward of the Writer's Plantations—A Second Shipment of Convicts and Arms for St. Christopher's Island—List and Particulars of the Malefactors.

LETTER XCIX.

To Captain James Phipps, a planter of St. Christopher's Island. Dated from London, 2 March, 168⅘.

Touching freights, cargoes and prices. The writer has instructed a person to dispose of the mollasses sent to the port of London by Captain Roberts, but cannot yet say what can be done with it. The sugar (ten hogsheads) sent to the writer by Ensign Thorn, is of so poor a quality that it will barely fetch 18s. for the hundred, instead of 19s. or 20s. "There are," adds the writer, "little alterations here since the great one which I advised you of in my last. Crowds of addresses dayly swarme into the court to condole for our loss, and to congratulate King James on his happy accession to the throne of his auncestors. There are great preparations for a parliament, which is to assemble at Westminster on the nineteenth of May. There will be great struggles about the elections. I pray God give a happy issue to their proceedings."

LETTER C.

To Ensign Edward Thorn, the Writer's agent and steward in St. Christopher's Island. Dated from London, 9 April, 1685.

A long letter dismissing Mr. Thorn from his office of steward to the writer, who begins his prolix and sometimes grandiloquent letter thus, "Ensign Thorn; you cannot thinke it strainge that I should revoke that power which you have so much abused; and I protest it has not been without some difficultie and conflict with myselfe, that I have taken up this resolution of putting my concernes into other handes; and tho' I am sensible of the too great reason I had to do it long since, yet the doing of it is to me no small dissatisfaction. I wish those severe letters, which produced only your complaintes, had so farre answered the desired ends as to have prevented the occasion of this greater breach between vs." With perfect truth and needless grandeur of diction, the writer observes that " carelessnesse is a certaine compagnion of profuseness," and that "those two locusts" have devoured his revenues, without enriching the agent, who is at length required to make room for a more worthy officer. " The gentleman," says the writer of the epistle, " I now send (for so I must call him, having known him near these twenty yeares to be such) will, I hope, approve himselfe to be such in all his actions, and chiefly in submitting to his fortune and living answerably to it, without injury to his employer. . . . . I desire you without compulsion to deliver up to him my plantation, with all the slaves, horses, and cattell, and all other goods and things thereon or thereunto belonging, as well moveable as immoveable, and all books and papers belonging to me or my concernes, with an exact and just accompt of all my estate."

LETTER CI.

To Colonel Hill, Governor of St. Christopher's Island. Dated from London, 13 March, 168⅘.

Showing that the Colonel's friendly feeling for the writer has been followed by a coldness, in consequence of the malicious misrepresentations referred to in previous letters. Protesting that he has acted with perfect frankness and punctilious honour towards the Governor in all matters relating to the transportation of malefactors, the writer entreats for a renewal of the cordial understanding between himself and his correspondent. It does not appear precisely in what way the Colonel conceives himself to be injured; but the fair inference from the writer's protestations is that he is suspected of having obtained too much advantage for himself in the arrangements about the convicts. The writer continues, " Mr. Recorder has several tymes demanded a certificate of the landing of those malefactors on the Island of St. Christopher's; and now Captain Richardson declares in open court that he dares aver they were never transported, which makes me very desirous to heare of their arrival. There are fourty odd men and women, who I hope will follow with others to St. Christopher's. I have not seen them, but have a character of them, that they are a parcel of likely young men. I have spoken about them to Mr. Recorder, who says their pardon will be pleaded on the twentieth of this moneth, and then we may have them on discharging the prison fees. The French are fitting out a squadron of shipps to be commanded by the Count d'Estrées; but all things are peaceable and quiet and in good order. The King and Queen will be crowned at Westminster, on the 23rd of April, being St. George's Day, and on the 19th of May the Parliament is to assemble. Some of the burgesses are already chosen, and it is hoped that the major part of them will be very loyal men. Several of the horse-guard are dead within this week or fortnight, and some others, of an ill feavour, upon which they are removed to the Mews, where they now do duty. This has caused some apprehensions of a sicknesse this summer."

LETTER CII.

To Captain Willett, a planter of St. Christopher's Island. Dated from London, 13 March, 168¾.

Giving a very unfavourable account of the sugar (ten hogsheads) which is so bad as to be fit only for the distillers. The highest offer as yet made for it is 17s. per cwt, whereas the best sugars are selling for 20s. and even 22s. the hundred. "Sir Nathaniell Johnson," the writer continues, "stands for parliament man. Several elections are already made; and the Parliament is to meete upon the 19th of May, if no contagion prevent, as is feared, by reason of a pestilential feavour, which is much discoursed of to be very mortal. The King and Queen are to be crowned at Westminster, on St. George's Day, the 23rd of April. There are provisions making for the solemnity, but it will be performed as privately as possible, and with as little charge, as maybe. The Queen of Denmarke is lately dead; so that now allmost all Christendome is in mourning."

LETTER CIII.

To Colonel Hill, Governor of St. Christopher's Island.

[Indicating a restoration of all former friendliness between the writer and his correspondent, this curious letter also indicates the cause of the colonel's transient dissatisfaction. It was consistent with the stinginess of the civic authorities that, whilst insisting on the payment of their exorbitant fees, and providing no escort for the safe conduct of the malefactors from Newgate to the river, they would not even throw their shackles and handcuffs into the bargain.— J.C.J.]

London, 28 March, 1685.

Your Honor's most welcome letter of the 24th of January by Captain Chant, I received the last night, for which I give your honour many thanks.

The letters, which some merchants received on the 28th of January, making no mention of the arrival of Captain Size, we began to feare all was not well with him; and last Saturday being at the Old Bayley to justify ourselves from some aspersions which Captain Richardson had cast upon us, the Lord Mayor seemed much dissatisfied with vs, because we had no certificate, or account of the landing of the men at St. Christopher's Island. But the whole businesse is that the persons, whose interest it is to oppose vs, spare no clamours, raise all objections, and make all the interest they possibly can against us, to prevent our taking off the present parcel; in order to which we did agree with one Captain Foster, master of the ship 'Friend's Goodwill,' for the passage of thirty odd men and eleven women, who we expect will be delivered to us; we discharging the prison fees and taking all the parcel indifferently, one with another, as it is enjoyned us. By which means the whole concerne is of so little value, considering the many considerable risques we run in this, more than other ventures, that, were it not for the service of his Majestie, and the advantage of the Island, rather than of ourselves, it would be our interest to desist from the undertaking.

Two days since by appoyntment we were to attend Sir Thomas Jenner, the City Recorder, with our securities, to give bond for the transportation of fourty-three or four persons which are under sentence of transportation. But before we entered upon this new matter, I *discoursed with Mr. Baxter of his unkindnesse, telling him that if your letters to him seemed dissatisfied at your being concerned, but a third share*, I was (as I offered the time before) now very willing to relinquish all or any part of my interest in it, for your Honour's satisfaction. But, my proposals not being accepted, we are again to be concerned as formerly, your

Honour one third, Mr. Vickers a third, and myselfe a third. We have given order for the making twenty-five payr of shackles, and as many handcuffs. We design to send with them armes as with the former parcel.

I was this morning to wait on the Earl of Feversham at his *levée*, to acquaint him that Mr. Vickers was suddainly bound away, and that he would wait on his Lordship next Saturday, to receive his commandes for St. Christopher's. He sayd he intended to write by him, and so doth Colonel Worden. I despaire of sending over Mr. Addy's brother, he having of late fallen in with so goode businesse, that he will scarce hearken to the proposal of such a voyage. Nor is his brother, Mr. Addy, inclined that he should.

These malefactors are likely to be dearer to vs than the last. We are to pay four pounds ten shillings for everyone's passage, besides the irons, and the doctor's fee, which was partly excused in the last lot. Though I fear Captain Size will expect we should consider his doctor at his retourne, as we did in a manner promise we would.

The fears we had of a contagious distemper are, blessed be God, past over. The Horse Guards will not retourne to their old Court de Guard, but continue to do duty at the Mews, till the guard-house by the Park be well cleaned, and ayred, and new-whited, which is now being done. The Queen has been very ill. Great preparations are making for the coronation of their Majesties. The French are forming a fleet at Brest, and have drawne a considerable body of an army into the neighbourhood of Calais. The French designes are not known, are supposed to be only to possess our people with fears and jealousies. There is little news stirring. You may expect Mr. Vickers soon after the receipt of this; for he designes to imbarque within this fortnight or sooner, as he says. I am commanded to joyne my sister's with my owne commendations of our humble services to your Honour, to your lady and sister, and to Mrs. Windall, with our hearty prayers for the long continuance of your health and happiness. CHRISTOPHER JEAFFRESON.

LETTER CIV.

To Captain Willett, a planter of St. Christopher's Island.
6 April, 1685.

Thanking the captain for the trouble he has taken in the writer's West Indian affairs, and begging him to act in conjunction with Mr. Vickers, under a letter of attorney, herewith conveyed to him by Mr. Sedgewick, the gentleman who is appointed to succeed Mr. Thorn in the management of the writer's plantations. It is remarked that the agreement between the writer and Mr. Thorn was for four years, a term not yet expired; but that the proprietor is justified morally as well as legally in setting aside this contract, in consideration of his servant's breach of nearly every covenant of the indenture. After alluding to the injuries he has sustained through Mr. Thorn's "idle and debauched course of life," the writer admits the sufficiency and merit of the water-work built on his property under the delinquent's supervision. But even in respect to this one creditable feature of his administration of the plantations, Mr. Thorn was not free from fault, as his procrastination in constructing the work occasioned his employer the loss of what promised to be a large and valuable crop of canes.

LETTER CV.

To Colonel Hill, Deputy-Governor of St. Christopher's Island. Dated from London, 9 April, 1685.

Asking the deputy-governor to grant his warrant to Mr. Sedgewick, the writer's newly-appointed steward, to take possession of the writer's plantations, and to "seize upon all papers, books and writings, as well as all goods and chattells, moveable and immoveable, which shall be on the sayd plantation." The story of Mr. Thorn's offences is told yet again; and with respect to the new water-work, of which he talks so much, as though it were a service which compensated for all his misdemeanours, it is observed that "he was well advised to make a water-worke, which, knowing the age of his canes and the workmen he was to employ, he should have begun six months sooner, to have saved my owne canes, and prevented the clamours of my tenants."

LETTER CVI.

To Major Crispe, a planter of St. Christopher's Island. Dated from London, 10 April, 1685.

Begging the Major to advise and assist the writer's new steward, Mr. Sedgewick, in all just proceedings, should he encounter opposition from Mr. Thorn, who, the writer suspects " has made two friends for one that he has lost."

LETTER CVII.

To Colonel Hill, Governor of St. Christopher's Island.

London, 18 April, 1685.

Sir.—I have tyme only to give your Honor a short accompt of the malefactors, which I sende by this ship 'The Friend's Goodwill,' Captain James Foster, master; with two chests of armes, viz., thirty swords and belts, and cartouche-boxes, and as many fire-lock musquets, of the same cost and price as the last were of, with sea-beds, cloathes, &c., convenient. But, for that we understood that the last parcel threw off their cloathes overboard, and came as bare to the island, as if they had had no cloathes, we thought good to save some of that charge, as you will see by the accompt.

I have informed your Honor formerly, how the women are forced upon us, and as it happens, the proportion this time is greater, considering the number of men, than in the last. I pray God they may all come well to the island, for they are a chargeable as well as troublesome sort of merchandize. The risque we run of escapes, mortality and other accidents is more than in all the rest. And now, tho' I have presented the certificate of delivery of the last, I cannot prevail with Mr. Recorder to deliver up our first bonds, which is hard measure. Captain Size tells me of one John Barnett, who was seen (after he was delivered, as being one of the first parcel) to have forty guinneys (as the boatswain affirmes that he saw); which, if the story be true, may make way for the escape not only of himselfe, but also of some of his fellows.

Mr. Vickers took shipping the sixteenth

instant. He is gone by the way of Barbadoes in the ship 'Industry,' Captain Pelly, commander; and Colonel Nethaway is gone by a Jamaica ship, which is to put him ashoar at Nevis. We are concerned in these convicts as in the last parcel, viz., your Honour a third, Mr. Vickers a third, and myselfe a third. There are two new charges upon these, that is, the chirurgeon's fees and the irons. But as for the shackles they may be sold in the island, and it maybe to profit; but we cannot well be losers by them, if they go off only as olde iron. I must be more particular in my next; for tyme will not allow me now to add any more, but my humble service to Your Honour and to Mrs. Windall.

CHRISTOPHER JEAFFRESON.

CHAPTER XV.

REBELLION.

(April, May, June, July, 1685.)

Another Rogue's March—Sir William Stapleton's Arrival—A Loyal and Liberal Parliament—Sir James Russell's Illness—Purchase of Negroes—Argyll's Rebellion—Arrests in the West of England—The Western Rising—The case of Lord Macclesfield and Mr. Fitton—Birth of a Princess—Monmouth and Grey in London—The Duke's Execution and Burial—Triumphal Return of the Guards—New Levies—More Prisoners from the West—Disposal of Regiments—Pursuit of Ferguson.

LETTER CVIII.

To Colonel Hill, Deputy Governor of St. Christopher's Island.

London, 22 April, 1685.

My letter to your Honour of the 18th instant being writ in haist, as I supposed that the master would, according to his promesse, have set sayle from Gravesend, so soon as we had put the malefactors on board his ship, I have made use of his delay in some measure to supply the defects of that letter.

Upon Easter Eve, about six of the clock, I went to Newgate to receive the malefactors, which ought to have been forty-seven in number; but two men and one woman were dead, and one man and a woman were sick. For several reasons and pretentions four men were deteyned. So that we had delivered to us but thirty-eight prisoners, viz., twenty-nine men (most of them sturdy and rugged fellows), and nine women (likely to make good servants). But I cannot understand that any of these men are of any trades or professions worthy giving an accompt of; only excepting Thomas Smith, a handsome, stout young man, who is a barber-chirurgeon, and is to be valewed as two others. William Pierce, a sickly man, is a chirurgeon, and has used the sea. There are about seven of them which have followed sea-affairs, and will make Captain Foster watchful in the voyage, and the masters of the shallops careful of their boats when they are upon the island. Captain Foster will inform your Honour of their names; but if he should talk of it on the island, it might hinder the sale of them,— for nobody, I suppose, will be desirous to buy a servant that has that convenience of freeing himself, by the first boat he can steal. John Walker says he is a shoemaker. Silvan Morris was a soldier, condemned for killing his comrade. Henry List is a weaver. Francis Abraham is a cook. These, with the mariners, are all the men with professions I know. But Captain Foster may discover more of their good qualities on the voyage. But they certainly are a parcel of as notorious villaines as any that have been transported this long tyme. I beg your Honour, when they are arrived, to dispatch your certificate away by the first ship, under your Honour's hand and seal, with the master's affidavit of misfortunes at sea, if any should happen to dye in the voyage, as is not improbable.

We have committed one great error in not putting shoes on board for them, which was occasioned by means of a dispute we had with our slopseller about the price, upon which we not agreeing, they are like to be a company of bare-footed soldiers. Tho' I thinke some of them are well provided with shoes, as well as cloathes. As they went down to the water-side, notwithstanding a guard of about thirty men, they committed several thefts, snatching away hats, perrewigs, &c., from several persons, whose curiosity led them into the crowd. They were all searched when they came on board; but what was found about them the captaine best knows, for it being Easter-day in the morning, I went no farther than the bridge with them, thinking the barges sufficiently armed. I ordered the masters to make the prisoners believe I was always at hand with a guard (if occasion should be), which kept them in awe.

I had to pay the fees for thirty-nine persons; but finding one of the women to be sicke and infirme I resolved to leave her behind, which the keepers were very angry at; and I could not prevail with them to retourne me the £1 11s. payd for her; which I chose rather to lose than to hazard the loss of five pounds more upon a sickly woman. I had some assistance when Mr. Vickers was with me; but now, being by myself, I did as well as I could, but with no small difficulty.

Captain Freeman, and the persons concerned with me, persuade me to desist for the future. But I hope it is a good piece of service to the island, if of little or no good to ourselves; and when Sir William Stapleton arrives, I designe to discourse his Excellency concerning it, whose interest, if he please, may remove most of the considerable obstacles that stand in our way. All matters relating to the islands are deferred till his coming; which hath prevented my serving the publick of the island, as otherwayes I should have endeavoured, and therefore I have forborne to write to the Council.

The bill of loading for the malefactors is inclosed in a letter, which I delivered to Captain Foster's own hand. They are all consigned to your Honour, to whom the whole disposal of them is referred; and I have not given order to any other persons to be concerned on my behalf, not doubting but that he, who manages my interests on St. Christopher's, will be ready at your Honour's command to perform anything that you shall see necessary to be done in the businesse; and supposing your Honour will make a receiver and order the shipping of the produce of the servants on a joynt accompt, to be so disposed of, and no division to be made in this concerne till the effects be reduced to money; which is my desire. I think it is the fairest and easiest expedient for the satisfaction of all parties, that the servants should be all sould upon a joynt accompt, and that the goods be received, shipped, and consigned to some one man in London, to be disposed of on a joynt accompt, and then a dividend be made of the moneys, when received according to an equal proportion, to each of us concerned, or to the assignees of any of us.

CHRISTOPHER JEAFFRESON.

A list of the names of the convicts shipped

on board The 'Friend's Goodwill,' Captain James Forster, Commander, April the 19th, 1685.

Richard Enos.	John Bourne.
Christian Bromfield.	Jane Arnex.
Mary Voyse.	Joseph Key.
John Pell.	Thomas Williams.
John Fuller.	Silvanus Morris.
Barbara Williams.	Mathew Harwat.
John Thoroughgood.	Catherine Cotterill.
John Morgan ap Hall.	Francis Abraham.
Dorcas Morgan.	George Clarke.
John Nerrop.	Henry List.
William Fincham.	Ralph Harrison.
Mary Reeves.	Thomas Stevenson.
John Walker.	William Williams.
Edward Perkins.	John Clutton.
John Wallbanck.	William Clarke.
Henry Curley.	Elizabeth Townsend.
William Temple.	Roger Adams.
William Butler.	Thomas Smith, chi-
Thomas Vickars.	rurgeon.

William Pierce, chirurgeon.

Since the writing this letter, I have prevailed with Captain Richardson for the

£1 11s., which was over-payd; on condition I shall not trouble them for the man if he recovers; nor is the woman to be imposed on us. Captain Den is arrived by whom I have received the second certificate and the duplicate of your Honour's letter by Chant.

LETTER CIX.

To Major Crispe, a planter of St. Christopher's Island.

London, 6 June, 1685.

Sir.—Having received a most obliging letter from you by Captain James Phipps, I was impatient of this opportunity of retourning my thanks for this and all your other courteous favours; to whom I am so great a debtor, that I cannot but blush to see myselfe treated with such civil and courtly expressions, so far beyond my merits.

The condition of my plantation is so natural a consequence of an imprudent, and carelesse management, that I could not in reason hope for better. It was never my order or design, that it should be left so bare of hands, and I kindly accept your good advice of putting on more slaves; which advice I so far applaud that I have taken order for a supply of negroes.

Sir William Stapleton and all our friends, that were the compagnions of his voyage, are in good health at present. I am told that last night a great difference happened between Captain Pogson and Captain Freeman. But, if you please, take no notice of it, unless you hear of it from other handes. Our General is very well received by the King, and will probably make his enemies ashamed of the injustice they have done him in his absence.

The Parliament is now sitting, and has given such demonstrations of loyalty, that we may now hope to be as happy a people as ever. They have settled the revenue and are giving a further supply, which will be very considerable, towards the recruiting of the stores, the repairing of the fleet, and the maintaining of peace at home and abroad. The funds, proposed for this supply, are an imposition, as formerly, on wines and vinagre, and upon salt, and an excise upon all sorts of sugars aud tobacco, that shall be consumed in the kingdom. But we have great hopes this latter will not pass. For all persons concerned are very diligent in making friends to oppose it when it comes to a debate. I hope his Majestie is now well satisfied that it is not for his interest, which if he be, we are well. The proposal was made by a Privie Councillor; and Mr. Blathwait says it will pass into an Act. The bill is not yet brought in, and never an Act has passed but that for the revenue. Yesterday was read a bill which the Lords sent down to reverse the judgment given against the Lord Stafford; against which proceeding some of the Lords protested. And another bill came down and was made, whereby it will be made felony for any person to marry a maid under fourteene or a man under sixteene, without the consent of the parents or guardians. Some are of opinion it will not pass. His Majestie's forces have not met with the rebels in Scotland; but are in pursuit of them. I hear of little or no disturbance in England; and I pray God to send vs in all parts peace, &c., &c., CHRISTOPHER JEAFFRESON.

LETTER CX.

To Colonel Hill, Deputy Governor of St. Christopher's Island.

London, 6 June, 1685.

Sir.—I have scarce had an opportunity of writing to your Honour since Captain Foster sailed with the second parcel of convicts, nor of answering your letter, which I received by Captain Phipps on the 10th of May; who arrived about that tyme.

Sir William Stapleton is well recruited since his arrival, as to his health. Sir James Russell haith been ill, but is in a good way of recovery; Captain Pogson has been visited with the gout, but walks abroad. His two daughters have had the small-pox, but are well again. So is Mrs. Betty Russell, who has had the like distemper. Mr. Lattee had a fit of illness on his first coming to London, but now he and all his friends are in perfect health.

I have delivered your letter to the Royal African Company; and at a court held at the African House upon Thursday the 28th of May, it was read, and an order was made upon it that a ship should forthwith be hired to answer the contents of it. As to other businesse, relating to the Islands, there has been very little done, in regard that the Parliament is sitting, and the King is full of the immediate businesse. The House of Commons have appeared very loyal, and seem willing and ready to do whatsoever his Majestie is pleased to require at their handes. They are preparing a bill to lay three farthings upon white sugars and one upon Muscovados, to be raised as an excise on what is consumed in the kingdom. It will be and has been most vigorously opposed. Some say the designed imposition is a halfpenny on Muscovados, and so rising till it comes to a groat on the best whites. But nothing is certain, the bill not being brought into the house; and when it is, I hope it will not pass. If I am not mistaken it will meet with a great many opposers, especially when the petition is delivered in with the printed paper of objections, which are ready and attend only the first reading of the bill.

We are daily in expectation to heare of the defeat of Argyle's party by his Majestie's forces; but he has found a way to escape them, and has marched into Galloway; not being then four or five thousand strong, as is reported. But if they were more, there is a powerful army attending their motions. Several persons have been apprehended in the West of England upon some suspitions of a riseing designed thereabout. And some of the Lord Argyle's letters have been intercepted, which discover his designs. A messenger, that went downe to take Mr. Trenchard into his custody, coming to Mr. Speake's house to demand him, was set upon by forty or fifty men, who beate him severely and carried off Mr. Trenchard. It is reported that a ship with four or five thousand armes on board was the other day chased into Poole by Sir Francis Wheeler, Captain of the Tyger frigate. His Majestie has a letter of it, but, it seems, from such handes that the truth of it is doubted of.

The Lord Macclesfield had yesterday a great hearing with Mr. Fitton before the House of Lords, and his decree was confirmed; nobody of the Lords speaking for Mr. Fitton. The Princesse Ann of Denmarke is delivered of a daughter, a very little one, &c., &c.,

CHRISTOPHER JEAFFRESON.

LETTER CXI.

To Mr. Lewis of Glamorganshire, the Writer's brother-in-law.

London, 18 July, 1685.

Deare Brother.—. . . . . When I had resolved to break away from my law-suits, and to begin my vacations at the latter end of this moneth, new matters are started up, which deny me the needful freedom. I meet with troubles where I expected none, insomuch that I cannot yet propose the tyme when I may leave the town without great inconveniency and prejudice to my affaires as they now lye. But my inclynations leade me to make what dispatch I possibly can, that I may have the satisfaction of seeing you before the summer be past [which is now declyning a-pace), and I shall endeavour it as soon as may be.

Mr. Gibbon's brother is now out of town. He lives with one Lieutenant Ely, and is made a serjeant to his company of dragoons. I have not sent you the Gazets, there being nothing in them worth the charge of the postage; only in Monday's is the proclamation for a thanksgiving for the late victory, on Sunday the 26th instant.

On Monday last, Monmouth and Grey were brought with a German, prisoners to White Hall, where they continued some five hours, and were admitted to the king's presence; the river being all the tyme thronged with boats about the Privy Stayers. Between seven and eight of the clock, they were carried in the King's barge to the Tower, whence upon Wednesday last, the Duke of Monmouth was brought to a scaffold on Tower Hill; the Bishops of Ely, and of Bath and Wells, Dr. Tennison, and the Dean of Ripon being present, who gave this account of his behaviour (as I was tould by one that had it from his mouth): That he was very resolute and unconcerned; That he sayd that he had sold his life for these two years past; That he believed this was the occasion of the cheerfulleness that he found upon his spirits, who, though he was in his nature timorous, yet now went as cheerfully to his death as ever he did to his dinner. He professed himself a Protestant of the Church of England; upon which, being informed that it was against the Articles of our Church to resist lawful authority, he sayd he believed them all. Then, it being tould him that it was a fit opportunity to exhort the people to obedience, he replied that he did not come there to make speeches. He sayd further that there was a certain lady of quality, that had suffered very much in her reputation on his accompt, the Lady Harriet Wentworth by name, who, if the word of a dying man may be believed, (sayd he), 'is a very virtuous lady, betweene whom and me no crime has ever been committed.' Mr. Sheriff asked if he was ever married to her. He replyed it was no time to answer questions. He joyned with the bishops in the publick prayers, but used no private devotions; and because he would not make a clear confession and recantation of the crimes for which he was to dye, the clergy refused him the sacrament. The leave that he took of his duchesse, who was with his two sons in the Tower, was very cold.

All people (that I can meet with) that saw him dye, say he carried himself very evenly without the least show of concern. He tryed the block, and the edge of the axe, and desired the executioner not to put him to torture, and gave him six guinneys in his hand, and four more in another's hand, in case he should do his work well. Being layd down, after some time he received a stroke; which making but a small gash, he raised his head a foot at least from the block, and looked on the executioner, then, lying down again he received two more strokes in the same place. Then Ketch flung down the axe and sayd he could not do it. But, being constrained to take it up again, he gave him two more, and then with his knife cut the flesh asunder. So that he had five strokes at him before he used his knife. His body was put in a coffin, and layd in the Tower Chappel.

The Lord Grey is very cheerful and jocose, saying that he did not expect to live when he came into England, and that nothing troubles him but his being esteemed a coward; whereas, when he saw he could not bring on or rally the horse, he went through the thickest of the battle to find out Monmouth, with whom he tarried till the fight was over. The Duke of Monmouth delivered a paper to the Sheriff for the King, the contents of which I know not.

Yesterday the detachments of the King's two regiments of Guards returned to London, bringing with them the trophies of their victories; 22 colours of the enemies borne by the men that took them, and blue foot-colours, and one horse colour, on which were in letters of gold these wordes 'Feare nothing but God.' Yesterday all the persons imprisoned in the Halls were set at libertie without bail. The levies for horse and foot go forward; but the new raised foot are already reduced to 60 in a companie, and so I think they will be established, and be dispersed in most of the counties of England. The Princesse is gone this morning for Tunbridge to drink the waters. On Thursday night several prisoners were brought to towne;—one Williams, the Duke of Monmouth's servant, a fanatick parson, and several others. The English and Scotch regiments from Holland have leave to retourne; only some of them will be tryed at a General Court Martial for seditious words. The Irish regiment is likewise ordered back for Dublin, so that now we may hope for peace and quiet; which God of his mercy grant us! We daily expect to hear that Ferguson is taken. They were in close pursuit of him, in so much that he quitted his horse near Ilford Coomb. Monmouth and Grey have given him the character of a most bloudy villain. I hope he will be taken, and all such firebrands and incendiaries of the rebellion.

Your affectionate brother,

CHRISTOPHER JEAFFRESON.

CHAPTER XVI.

THE LATE TROUBLES.

(August, 1685.)

West Indian Markets—Peter De Grave's Death—Argyll's Rising—His Execution—Monmouth's Insurrection—Military Movements—Facts not published in the Gazettes—The Battle of Bridgewater—The Earl of Arlington, Lord Chamberlain—The Earl of Feversham—The Lords Stamford, Delamere and Brandon in the Tower—Changes in the Army—The Duke of Albemarle—Lord Churchill—Ensign Matthew—Gaols full of Rebels—St. Christopher's Island asking for a Cargo of Rebels.

LETTER CXII.

To Ensign Matthews, a planter of St. Christopher's Island. Dated from London, 4 August, 1685.

Acknowledging the arrival in London of ten tuns of Muscovado sugar, and three tuns of molasses, which the Ensign has consigned to the writer, for sale in the London market. Expressing his gratification at this proof of Mr. Matthews's undiminished confidence in and friendship for him, the writer regrets that he is "so pestered with lawsuits and other businesses," as to be quite unable to execute the commission. In his inability to look after the matter himself, the writer has transferred the commission to "Messrs. Sympkin and Wrayford, men that you know to be of very honest repute, and well experienced in those affairs." As he employs Messrs. Sympkins and Wrayford as brokers for the disposal of his own West Indian products, the writer does no better for himself than he now does for his friend. "Your brothers and friends here," he continues, "are all well, excepting poor Peter De Grave, who, to the great regret of all who knew him, is dead of the small-pox, which has been very fatal and epidemic this summer, more so, I think, then ever I knew it. Or at least the effects of it have been more grievous to me. For besides this good friend, Mr. De Grave, I lost two or three days since a near kinsman, the hope and prop of his family, just ready to heir an estate of £500 per annum, and *that* by this unfortunate distemper. I bless God, I have hitherto escaped it; but several of my acquaintance have had it this summer. Sir James Russell is just recovered of it; but I fear he will lose his youngest daughter that is here."

LETTER CXIII.

To Colonel Hill, Governor of St. Christopher's Island.

London, 5 August, 1685.

Honoured Sir.—I lately saw a note written by Captain Foster to Mr. Baxter, importing that he was thrown on shore at Antegoa, and that he had sent down all the malefactors to St. Christopher's excepting three, which he made use of to save his goods.

I perceive that the planters were very shy of buying the first parcel of malefactors; they not being all disposed of when these arrived, and those that were disposed of, having proved so troublesome to their masters, that I am doubtful these will come to a bad market; and now sugars are so low, and the impositions so high, that it will be well if we ever see our own money for them, and yet I perceive the planters are very backward in the payment for those they have had.

I had made this progress in my letter, when yours and Mr. Smith's came to my hands, giving me the best assurance that can be of the landing of twenty-five of our servants by Captain Foster on St. Christopher's. I am sorry for that captain's loss. Probably we shall be sharers in it. The arms, if not lost, will be spoyled, which is sufficient to destroy the voyage. Thank God it is no worse, but the certificate you have been pleased to send us will be only a satisfaction to ourselves; and will not avail us, for the taking up of our bonds. For they are so scrupulous here, that they require the person bringing the certificate, under your hand and seal, to make oath before one of the Barons of the Exchequer, that he saw it signed and sealed, which Captain Size did, and upon that with much ado we got our first obligation cancelled by the Recorder of London, who keeps it with the certificate affixed to it. . . . . . .

The small-pox has been extremely rife and mortal this year. But, I thank God, the feares we had of a contagion were soon removed. It haith pleased God, within the space of five or six months, to give us a sight of some of his dreadful judgments, which, tho' we justly deserved them, He in mercy haith most miraculously delivered us from them. May it be His good pleasure to make us truely sensible of them, and thankful for them, so that we may no more provoke him to anger!

In the month of May last, the troubles began in Scotland. Archibald Campbell, the late Earl of Argyle, who for policy and conduct as well as great personal valour was no contemptible rebel, landed in the West of Scotland amongst a disaffected, unfaithful people, who in no small numbers joyned with the party he brought with him in three ships from Holland; in so much that the rebellion began to grow considerable; and then by the providence of God more than the wit of men, being misled by their own guides, they were dispersed, and so became an easie prey to the King's force, who prest them hard before, and were commanded by the Lord Dunbarton and the Marquess of Athol, who behaved themselves with much prudence and courage in all the actions, that passed during the civil war, which lasted scarce a month. Argyle was taken and beheaded: Rumbold was hanged; and Ayliff, after ripping up his belly, is in a hopeful way of recovery towards a more shameful death. Many others are taken, and I suppose executed.

But the troubles, which happened in England at the same tyme, made us less inquisitive of the affaires of Scotland, when we understood the kingdome was in peace. For on Barnaby day, being the eleventh of June, the Duke of Monmouth, with three ships from Holland, landed at Lyme in Dorsetshire, with little or no resistance. The Mayor fled, and many of the towne joyned with the invaders, who were not above two or three hundred at the most that were landed, amongst whom were several old experienced officers. In a few days they took the field, and notwithstanding that the Duke of Albemarle was there with the militia, they marched to Taunton, where they greatly increased their numbers. Some of the Earl of Oxford's troops, and Colonel Churchill's dragoons were sent down, and in the skirmishes, that happened with various success, some few were slayne on both sides. But the Duke of Monmouth made short stays wherever he came. Passing through Somersetshire and Wiltshire, he came to Bath, but was not admitted into the towne; some of the King's forces appearing in sight of it, just as the demand was made. It was a detachment from the forces, sent down with the Earl of Feversham, who was General in this expedition. At Phillips-Norton was a bloody encounter. Many of the horse grenadiers were slayne; and the Duke of Grafton, showing too much heat and courage, had engaged his men too far amongst the enemy, who had lined the hedges, and did great execution, so that the Duke was in no small danger himselfe in the retreat.

Thursday's Gazet, July the 2nd, gives

some accompt of this action, but very favourably and partially, as I have been since informed. I have sent your Honour several other Gazets, which inform you of most particulars, as well of the Scotch as of the English rebellion. The rebels passed into Gloucestershire at Cansheime bridge, but a party of the King's forces, falling with some advantage on their rear, alarmed them, so that they repassed the bridge; after which they went to Wells and so to Bridgewater, where they seemed to fortify themselves. In the meanwhile, the Duke of Beaufort had secured the city of Bristol, confyning the most factious or suspected persons; and all over England the noted Whigs were imprisoned. Here in towne most of the city halls were filled with disaffected persons, or such as were so esteemed; and there was not a county in England free of the people who were inclined to aid the Duke of Monmouth. In several parts, especially Cheshire, here and in Hampshire, there was great cause of suspicion that the militia were not to be trusted;

several of them having made it appear that it was want of loyalty to their prince that made them loath to fight; for some of them showed great courage and resolution in a bad cause.

The rebels at Bridgewater were eight or ten thousand strong, and might have been much more, if they had not wanted armes and money. But the Earle of Feversham, with the King's forces, being come within three miles of the towne, Monmouth thought it necessary to flush his men with a victory, which he doubted not of obteyning. And indeed so great was his conduct, his vigilance, his indefatigable diligence, and so bold and numerous and resolute were his people, that the glory of the miraculous victory, must be rendered to God alone, who gave it to a small body of men, who were in a manner surprised in the dead of the night, which some made use of to escape the danger. But the private soldiers of the Lord Dunbarton's regiment, and of the King's foot-guards behaved themselves (as his Majestie since tolde them) like gallant men, and many of them were slayne. For the rebel foot fought desperately and made good fire, till the King's cannon, playing among them, made lanes through their body. I have heard the late Duke of Monmouth should say that, if his men had followed his orders, they could not have failed of victory:—that is, if his foot had not fired upon the out sentries, but had marched over the ditch, our foot would have been wholly surprised and overpowered with numbers; and if his horse, as was his orders, had fallen into Weston, they would have taken the cavalry in their quarters.

But Heaven spared us from those long and most bloudy wars, which in all probability would have been the fatal consequences of their success.

Their Majesties are gone for Windsor; and, the Earl of Arlington being dead, the Earl of Aylesbury is made Lord Chamberlain, and the Earl of Feversham Knight of the Garter. The Lord Grey and Monmouth were soon taken, though far from the place of battle, in a wood in Hampshire. I have sent you the accompt of Monmouth's execution, at which you may perceive he did not appear so good a christian as he had showed himself a soldier. Several of the rebels are taken; and Richard Goodenough, it is sayd, confesses. The Lord Stamford, Delamere and Brandon Garrett* are in the Tower, and several others are inquired after, who were not actually in armes. The Duke of Albemarle has taken some distaste, and has layd down all his commands. I hear the Duke of Northumberland is to have the troop, and the Lord Churchill the Duke of Northumberland's troop. There are six regiments of new raised foot, and I think no less horse, to keep us quiet. Ensign Matthews behaved himself extraordinary well in the West, and was the only ensign of the officers of the six companies of the regiment that went down and kissed the King's hand upon their retourn. There were very few officers killed on the King's side, except in the Lord Dunbarton's company. Captain Chevalier was killed. The gaols are

* Charles Gerard, Lord Gerard of Brandon.—J.C.J.

full of prisoners, and some hundreds will be transported, but they are not yet condemned. I hope that St. Christophers will have a share of them. His Majestie has ordered that they shall be dispersed to several colonies. I have been several tymes at Whitehall and with Mr. Blathwait about them; desiring that the King would send some of them in one of his frygates to St. Christophers .... I pray you, give my humble service to your Lady and accept the same from,   Sir,

Your Honour's most faithful servant,
CHRISTOPHER JEAFFRESON.

Postscript.—The Earl of Feversham has the Duke of Albemarle's troop, and the Lord Churchill his. The Parliament met yesterday, and are adjourned till the 9th of November.

LETTER CXV.

To Mr. Vickers, a planter of St. Christopher's Island. Dated from London, 6 August, 1685.

After announcing Sir William Stapleton's arrival in England, and Mr. Peter De Grave's death, and touching on other matters set forth in previous letters of this collection, the writer says, " We have had a very troublesome season since your departure, England and Scotland being both embroiled in civil wars at the same tyme. The rebellions lasted in each kingdom neere a month, and, considering how formidable they grew, and what a noise they made in the little time, it is a miracle of mercy to see vs all now in peace. When I look upon the action of Bridgewater, where Monmouth was defeated, and think of the numbers of men (for the tyme, well disciplined, and very resolute) on the rebels side, who were led with admirable conduct even to surprise a small body of the King's army in the dead of the night, I cannot but admire the great handywork of God, to give the victory to those few men, whose conduct, as themselves must confess, deserved not so good success. The courage of a great many are reflected upon (but I must not meddle with those particulars) whom success crowns. All the foot soldiers fought extremely well. The action lasted near an hour and half between the foot, but Monmouth's horse were ill mounted, and could not stand the shock; nor did they, as it is sayd, perform orders, which were to have fallen into a town called Weston, where they should have surprised the King's horse in their quarters; but Heaven prevented it, and by the disposal of this victory delivered us from a most bloudy war, which otherwise in a few days would in all probability have overspread the kingdome; the eyes of multitudes being fixed on their success at this battle. For the particulars I refer you to the papers I sent the Governor."

CHAPTER XVII.

PERSONAL AFFAIRS.

(17 *September* 1685 *to* 17 *November* 1685.)

Mrs. Lewis of Glamorganshire and Channell Row—Edward Thorn's preposterous Misconduct—Thames Water—The Treaty of Neutrality—Impudent Demands—Severity needful in governing Slaves—Escape of a Convict—The Writer's anxiety about Captain Foster—Countenance afforded by the Writer's Friends to his knavish Steward—Dilapidation and bareness of the Writer's House in St. Kitts.

LETTER CXVI.

To Colonel Hill Governor of St. Christopher's Island.

[*Note.*—The omitted passages of this letter relate to the arrival and departure of West Indian ships, the dishonest practices of Edward Thorn, the unsatisfactory sale of some of the sugars paid for the first lot of malefactors, and the writer's desire for a sufficient certificate of the arrival of the second party of convicts.—J. C. J.]

London, 27 October, 1685.

..... I am heartily glad to heare of your welfare, and that your Lady is so well recovered, to whom I beg the tender of my humble service, and that she may know my sister is her humble servant. When Madam Hill shall favour this clymate by a retourn hither, she will find my sister so far disposed to gratifie herself, as not to lose the happiness of her agreeable conversation, for whom she hath a particular esteem. My sister is not so retired into Wales, but that she also keeps her house in Channell Row (where I now am), designing to spend part of the year in her beloved London; which is according to the articles of marriage, which in such cases are seldom like the laws of the Medes and Persians. Her dwelling in Wales is in the best part of Glamorganshire, one of the finest counties of Wales, where she is so pleased, that she is easily prevailed upon to keep Christmasse there, designing to be in town before Easter.

Sir, I must acknowledge the obligation I have to your Honour for all your kindness to me and mine; and your good intentions to do me the justice I required. As I received a double injury from those gentlemen, who in dissuading your Honour implyed that I had requested something which in reason and justice could not be granted, I hope your Honour will give me leave at this distance to justifie myself, and to wipe off that aspersion. It is certaine your Honour knows how common and practicable it is in England for a landlord to enter forthwith not only upon his own but his tenant's stock, upon non-payment of rent, and if the seizure be not lawfully made, the tenant is left to his remedy at law or in Chancery. This is only to show that a man may be immediately dispossessed, who is upon such termes. But this is not my case. Mine is clearer. For no man can deny that, when an attorney's or bailif's power is recalled, he is a trespasser, and a good action lyes against him, if without leave he enter any more on the premises. Now that indenture, which some gentlemen (who spoke Mr. Thorn's language) were pleased to call the articles of agreement, had no longer life or force in it, than whilst the letter of attourney, to which it related, stood good and unrevoked.......

...... I fear Captain Foster designes to drink no more Thames water, or else he would have more regard to his obligations. It is not our interest to do him any injury in his reputation; but I must inform your Honour that Mr. Baxter tells me that he lyes under a very ill name amongst the merchants. He confesses he was deceived in him, but I could not hold declaring my opinion of him to Mr. Baxter. Before he went hence, his management was so idle and ambiguous in our concerns, that I did express my doubts of him, and indeed I much suspected that he would not have performed for us so well as he hath done. I am forced to speak very fair to Mr. Recorder till I have a certificate, attested by some one who can make oath to it that all the prisoners are landed on St. Christopher's Island.

The Treaty of Neutrality and several other matters relating to the interest of St. Christopher's and the other Islands, now lye before his Majestie. Sir William Stapleton who presented a memorial of them to the King, will, I doubt not, give your Honour a more perfect accompt of his proceedings and success in those matters than I can."

LETTER CXVII.

To Mr. Sedgewick, the Writer's agent and steward in St. Christopher's Island. Dated from London, 31 October, 1685.

Instructing Mr. Sedgewick at very great length how he is to proceed against Ensign Thorn, who obtained by some means early intelligence of Mr. Sedgewick's mission, and insists that, as a partner in the writer's West Indian business, he cannot be ejected from his office till the term of their four years' contract has come to an end. Mr. Sedgewick is told that, instead of yielding to

Ensign Thorn's menaces and accepting the hospitality of Mr. Vickars for six weeks, he should have taken possession of the house on the Wingfield Manor plantation, and have turned its present occupant out of doors. The writer is not surprised to learn from his correspondent that Mr. Thorn has made friends for himself by corrupt and fraudulent practices—for instance, by lending the writer's horses and cattle to persons whom he designed to attach to his interest. The new steward is also strenuously exhorted to provide abundance of provision for the fifty negroes and other servants committed to his authority, and to govern the negroes without recourse to the cruelty by which Mr. Thorn has distinguished himself. On the other hand, he must " keep a strict hand over them," as slaves must live in "awe" of him who would manage them rightly. He must be prepared for any and every possible exhibition of dishonesty and vindictive malice on the part of Ensign Thorn, who, to inflict further injury on a munificent employer, will perhaps incite the slaves to desert the plantation.

LETTER CXVIII.

To Ensign Edward Thorn, for some years the Writer's agent and steward in St. Christopher's Island. Dated from London, 31 October, 1685.

Replying to a letter in which Mr. Thorn assumed the part of a person much aggrieved by his late employer; this epistle is moderate and even kind in tone, but by no means deficient in firmness. The writer can no longer retain in his service the young man whom he has employed for nine years in one or another capacity; but he wishes him well, and in spite of past annoyances would render him assistance. The epistle is signed, "Sir, I remain

"Your constant friend,

"CHRISTOPHER JEAFFRESON."

LETTER CXIX.

To Mr. Vickers, a planter on St. Christopher's Island. Dated from London, 2 November, 1685.

Touching Mr. Thorn's conduct in resisting the newly appointed steward, and refusing to put him in possession of the writer's property. "I give you," says the writer, "many thanks for your kindness to Mr. Sedgewick in the voyage, and since his arrival at St. Christophers. I am much ashamed that he should be troublesome to you for the six weeks that Edward Thorn as impudently as unjustly keeps him out of possession of my house, where himself haith not the least right, nor anything to do there since I revoked his letter of attourney."

LETTER CXX.

To ——, a planter of St. Christopher's Island. Dated from London, 2 November, 1685.

Touching the behaviour of Mr. Thorn, who threatens to bring an action against the writer for wrongful dismissal and breach of contract. The writer laughs at this threat, calling it "a scarecrow," and is content that Mr. Thorn's partisans should think the Ensign a harshly-treated man, since the "gentlemen" of the island know the truth of the case.

LETTER CXXI.

To Colonel Hill, Governor of St. Christopher's Island. Dated from London, 5 November 1685.

Announcing the escape and return to England of one of the convicts, shipped to St. Christopher's Island in the first lot of malefactors. "I am now," says the writer, "to acquaint your Honour that one Jacob Watkins, *alias* Morgan, whom I sent over to St. Christopher's in the first parcel of convicts, is retourned hither, as I am informed by one who both saw him and spoke with him, and promises to discover for me in what ship he came over in; likewise how I may meet with him again." Passing to another matter which occasions him anxiety, the writer says, "I am tould that, if the men Captain Foster detains at Antigua be not sent down to St. Christopher's, I shall assuredly come into trouble, or if any of the last parcel of convicts should escape, and come over before our bonds are taken up, (which cannot be without an authentick certificate, well attested by one who can swear to the truth of it, and that he saw your Honour sign it.)" Sir William Stapleton being in London, the writer, of course, moves openly and on his own responsibility, in no matter affecting the general interest of St. Christopher's Island; but he takes occasion, from time to time, to remind the General of the needs of the colony.

LETTER CXXII.

To Mr. Sedgewick, the Writer's agent and steward in St. Christopher's Island. Dated from London, 9 November, 1685.

Touching the strange intelligence that the writer (if Mr. Thorn's assertions may be trusted) is in debt to Ensign Edward Thorn. "That the plantation," says the writer, "should be in his debt is no small surprise to me. I know he was poor when I left the island, (I fear much worse than nothing,) and, as he managed my interest, it could never be very profitable to him or me; besides, his expenses were so extravagant, that his allowance could never at best have maintained them." How, then, did Mr. Thorn obtain money to invest in the writer's estate?

LETTER CXXIII.

To Mr. Sedgewick, the Writer's agent and steward in St. Christopher's Island. Dated from London, 17 November, 1685.

Touching some of the details of the accounts which Mr. Thorn has prepared for his defence against claims which he anticipates from his late employer. Familiar though he is with Mr. Thorn's cleverness in winning sympathy and confidence, and also with the disposition of the West Indian colonists to advocate the cause of a resident against an absentee, without reference to justice, the writer is astonished and indignant at the countenance and protection afforded to the faithless steward by persons of influence in the island, who are well aware of his dishonesty. "I could," says the writer, "have never expected the opposition you met, or imagined I was so much forgotten by my friends in three years tyme. I perceive everybody that did appear on my behalfe was very tender of disobliging Mr.

Thorn and his considerable adherents, and very cautious of admitting any severity to be used for example's sake. If I had been there, it would have strangely altered the case with E. Thorn. Major Crispe and Ensign Matthew would not have been capable of justifying or maintaining his most unjust accounts. The Major writes to me by Mr. Hare these words, 'I would not have you so much as to thinke that Ensign Thorn's interest, or the friendship of the gentlemen here, can pretend to stand in competition with yours; and what respect the gentlemen have shewed him haith been in a great part on your accompt. I have just seen Mr. Sedgewick, and offered him my service.' I thought myself sure of him, at least, as a neuter; nor did I think any person would have openly appeared against so just a cause, nor anyone but Ensign Matthew would have stood vp so stifly against my interest, where I had right on my side."

Noticing Mr. Sedgewick's account of the state in which he found the plantation, the proprietor says, " I am heartily sorry that you came to so bare a plantation, and found the house so ill-furnished. I left a good feather-bed and boulsters, with blankets and sheets and a rug, which would have been fitter for your lodging than a hamack, wherein you are apt to take cold. I was not so circumspect as was necessary in making an exact inventory of everything I left in the house, as you would have found had you surprised him, as I intended you should. I left a stock of goats, fowls, and the like on the plantation when I came away, and I do not believe he lived there without such conveniencies, which were easily conveyed away at the news of your coming. He used my table-linen and dishes too often, else he and they might have lasted longer; but as for what is worn out I am content, seeing it was my folly to allow him the use of them on all occasions. But in my opinion he ought to have made good to me those things which, being in the inventory, have been lost by his carelessness. I gave him ten in a hundred to maintain him on the plantation, and as a sufficient salary for all his care, and never agreed to allow him anything for receiving my rents; that is a most unjust charge, contrary to the letter and sense of his indenture. He charges commission for the sale of one of the convicts to Lieutenant Munday; and in Mr. Vickars's accompt of the convicts, I am charged with 22,000 pounds of sugar received by E. Thorn, who in his accompts makes no allowance for it."

CHAPTER XVIII.

BUSINESS AND POLITICS.

(9 *December*, 1685 *to* 18 *January*, 1685-6.)

An Absent Partner—A Liberal Parliament—Sir William Stapleton and the Lords Commissioners—Pardons for Refusing the Test—Lord Anglesey's Indictment of Bernard Howard—Trial of Charles Gerard, Lord Gerard of Brandon—Lord Delamere, Sir Robert Cotton and Mr. Offley out on Bail—Amsterdam and the Prince of Orange—West Indian Morals—The Royal African Company—The French Fleet—Fire at Wapping—Bills of High Treason—Religious Persecution in France.

LETTER CXIV.

To Colonel Hill, Deputy-Governor of St. Christopher's Island, Dated from London, 9 December, 1685.

Expressing the writer's dissatisfaction that the sugar, paid as the price of convicts, should have been divided in the island, instead of being first sent to London and converted into money, according to the agreement of the three adventurers; and that four of the unsold convicts, being decrepid men, incapable of labour, should have been quartered on his plantation. From the letter, it appears that as an absentee the writer suffered at the hands of his intimate friends, Colonel Hill and Mr. Vickers, who, in the disposal of the malefactors, thought much for their own and not at all for their absent partner's interest. Still, it appears, that of the unsold convicts quartered on the writer's property, twelve were in good condition; consequently he had the advantage of their unbought labour, till they came to be sold. Respecting the settlement of his differences with Edward Thorn, the writer says, "I beg your pardon for all the troubles I gave you in my private concernes. I find I had many enemies and but few friends, concerned in the deciding the difference between me and my steward; and I wonder that my attourneys were so well satisfied with his accompt, as to suffer it to be allowed. Mr. Thorn's friends were more zealous for him than mine for me; otherwise, certainely he would not have been allowed his salary (only due upon condition) for starving my negroes, killing my horses and cattle by other men's work, and leaving the plantation in a far worse condition than when he first entered it."

Passing from private to public matters, the correspondent continues, "All is peace at home, excepting only some few remaines of the Western rebels, which are now gotten together in those parts again; and the peace with France is likely to continue. The Parliament, at their last sitting, enacted nothing, but voted a supply to His Majestie of £700,000 upon two funds, which would have made him neere double the sum; but some debates about officers that would not take the test, growing high, they were prorogued till the 10th of February; so nothing was done. The affaires of Sir William Stapleton's government now lye before the Lords Commissioners, and next Monday is appointed to be the day, but what may be hoped from this, when affaires are so unsettled and money so scarce,

I do not know. But our condition will lye before them, and if they will not answer our expectations, we may hope there is no danger of a war with France. However, I hope they will consider vs in some measure, seeing our necessities are so great. His Majestie hath granted his pardon to all the officers in commission that will not take the test; but the Lord Anglesey hath brought an indictment against Bernard Howard on the same accompt, which will be tryed the next terme. The Lord Brandon Gerrard* was tryed and condemned this terme for high treason; but his pardon, it is thought, will succeed his reprieve, which is granted. His father, the Lord Macclesfield, is fled beyond the sea. The Lord Stamford will be tryed by the House of Lords at the next Sessions. The Lord Delamere, Sir Robert Cotton, and Mr. Offley are out upon bail; it is reported that the chief evidence against them is desperately ill. The country people complaine much of the new army, but care is taken to redress those abuses.

* Lord Gerard of Brandon.—J.C.J.

The roads are full of robbers. The Lord Clarendon is going suddainely for Ireland as Deputy-Lieutenant. The Amsterdamers have submitted to the Prince of Orange, and acknowledged their error. So that at present there is a great union in Holland. The persecution in France is very cruel. The Germans and Venetians are victorious against the Turks."

LETTER CXXV.

To Mr. Sedgewick, the Writer's agent and Steward in St. Christopher's Island. Dated from London, 9 December, 1685.

Warning his steward against the demoralizing influence of persons whom he will necessarily encounter in his new position, and exhorting him not to yield to the immorality generally prevalent in West Indian society, the writer says, "My long experience of your good principles and virtuous inclynations leaves me no room for doubts or suspicions, that the evil example of prodigality or successful knavery should make any impression upon you. It is a common observation that the clymate, or rather the conversation of the people where you now are, does in a short tyme so influence most travellers who make any considerable abode there, that it extremely alters their manners and lessens their probity. I will not assert this hard and severe censure; having lived there sometyme myself, and having been acquainted with as honest men there as I have met with in the other parts of the world where I have lived. Those whose inclynation and discretion lead them to be just may be so there, as well as elsewhere. You will soon learn the nature of the people, and you have already found that the same breath blows hot and cold. You have the more reason to have a care whose counsel it is you walk by. Self-interest is the main wheel by which the mighty machine of this world's affaires is moved; some will advise you as my friends, some as if particularly your own, tho' at the same tyme they have no real kindness for either of vs, but aim at a private advantage and interest."

Contrasting the state of his plantation

when he left it, with its condition when Mr. Sedgewick entered it, the writer says, " I left Ensign Thorn my plantation in July, 1682, planted with many acres of young canes of my owne, besides my tenants, and a good quantity of young provisions, forty-six working slaves, a good cattle-mill and sugar-worke, with cattle, horses, and all necessary conveniences, as you see by the inventory, and since I came over I have sent him to the value of between two or three hundred pounds sterling in goods, and three servants; and yet he hath not paid the debts I left, which were not a hundred thousand pounds (sugar) more than was due to me on the island, and has created new ones which also are unpaid; and has not returned me so much sugar, as has cleared two hundred pounds, that is, it comes far short of paying the disbursements I have made here for the plantation. He has lost 12 or 13 of my slaves, several of my cattle, and almost all my horses, and leaves the plantation in great disorder; few canes in it, no provisions, and the very goods delivered by inventory lost, worn out, and destroyed. . . . . . I did not expect my house would have been left so bare to you. I am sorry I left my linen, pewter, and other necessaries to Edward Thorn, seeing he has made so ill use of them. I brought some pewter and table-linen with me, and some of that I left was good diaper, and not commonly used, and probably is not worn out. He took advantage of the tyme he was upon my plantation, after he knew of your power, to dispose of his stock, as I believe; for he would hardly kill the old goats that I left, which were breeders."

LETTER CXXVI.

To Mr. Vickers, a planter in St. Christopher's Island.

[*Note.*—The omitted passages of this letter related to the flagrant injustice of the decisions of the Commissioners appointed to arbitrate on and determine the disputes between Mr. Edward Thorn and the writer. —J. C. J.]

London, 15 December, 1685.

. . . . . . Colonel Hill writes me word that you have shipped home thirty thousand pounds of sugar (received by Mr. Mead in our joynt concern of the malefactors) in Captain Pelly, on your own proper accompt. I wish I had had some shipt to me also about that tyme when freight was cheaper than I can expect it the next year; but, if we fly off from our first agreement, it will create several difficulties and misunderstandings, which, by the due performance of it, might be avoided. I am sorry that any bad debts are made on this accompt. I hope by your next I shall hear better news of this concern; for I desire that either all the sugars received, or to be received, may be shipt and sold here on a joint accompt, as was at first agreed on, or else that my share may not be the last received, nor the last shipt home. I don't know what trouble Jacob Watkins may bring upon us by his escape. He is very bold, and appears publickly amongst the watermen below the bridge. I was once in chase of him.

The Royal African Company have made choice of Mr. Thomas Belchamber to be their agent, joyned with Mr. Carpenter, upon

Nevis, in Mr. Robert Helme's room. The French are fitting out a squadron of men-of-war at Brest and Rochefort for the West Indies; the Public News saith six frigates, the Private Intelligence speaks of fifteen. What the designe is I cannot imagine; but on this coast there is little likelihood of a breach with that crown, or any preparations that look like provisions for a war; and I believe it is the English interest to keep peace at home and abroad.

Last Thursday happened a fierce fire near the Hermitage at Wapping, which consumed in a few hours between thirty and forty houses. It was a very rainy night. Of late we have had several violent stormes on our coasts, which have injured the merchant ships; and several are perished on the coast of Holland. The Grand Jury of Cheshire have found a bill of high treason against the Lord Delamere, and of high misdemeanour against Sir Robert Cotton and Mr. Offley. The Lord Brandon Garret* has his pardon. The horrid persecution in France against the

* Lord Gerard of Brandon.—J.C.J.

poor Protestants continues with such unusual cruelties as have scarce been practised in any age I ever read of. Sir, I pray you give my service to your good lady and her sisters, to Mr. Dove and his lady, to Captain Willett and his lady, and be pleased to accept the same yourself from him that is, Sir,

Your obliged humble servant,
CHRISTOPHER JEAFFRESON.

Postscript.—Mr. Baxter is dead and buried this last week.

LETTER CXXVII.

To Mr. Sedgewick, the Writer's agent and steward in St. Christopher's Island. Dated from London, 19 December, 1685.

Reflecting on the egregious and often ludicrous dishonesty of Mr. Thorn's accounts, which the arbitrators have allowed, the writer observes that he is made to pay for the steward's "liveries" and also for his wearing apparel. Respecting the sale of whatever goods he may consign to his correspondent, to be disposed of in the island, the writer says, " Whenever I send you any goods to dispose of, it will be necessary in order to incourage neighbours and coustomers to come to the house, that you sell your commodities cheaper than the merchants who keep store-houses do afford them. For what is so vended may be allowed at an easier rate. That is only a hint I give you; but I would never send goods to create long debts. I had rather accept of the lesser profits and have a quick return." Mr. Sedgewick is also enjoined to get from Edward Thorn all the manuscripts which he was keeping for the writer, including the "Booke of the Ancient Orders of the Island,"

LETTER CXXVIII.

To Mr. Sedgewick, the Writer's agent and steward, in St. Christopher's Island. Dated from London, 18 January, 168⅘.

Instructing Mr. Sedgewick how to act in his final settlement of accounts with Edward Thorn, whose impudent knaveries are again exhibited to scorn; and how to deal with John Steele, the overseer, who must be regarded as in some degree accountable for Thorn's excesses.

CHAPTER XVIII.

LONDON AND THE LEEWARD ISLANDS.

(January, 1685-6.)

Impolitic Severity—The Committee for Trade—Alderman Lucy—Alderman Jefferys—Colonel Byar—West Indian Politics—Trial of Lord Delamere in Westminster Hall—Mr. Hambden guilty of Treason—Episcopal Changes—The Demand for the Principality of Orange—Madam Sydley, Countess of Dorchester—The Writer's reason for holding his West Indian Property in his own Hands—Anticipation of Civil Troubles—A Store opened at the Writer's House in St. Kitt's.

LETTER CXXIX.

To Mr. Vickers, the Writer's agent and steward in St. Christopher's Island. Dated from London, 20 January, 168$\frac{5}{6}$.

Dealing with matters of account, that afford no points of interest. The postscript of the not entertaining letter, however, is noteworthy: " The severe laws against the French inhabitants in the English quarter on St. Christopher's have in a great measure had the effects expected from them; but now, if the French persecutions should follow the Protestants into the Indies (as it is to be feared they will), those laws will affright them from taking sanctuary in the English part of the island, which might otherwise be much strengthened and improved thereby, as probably they would be true English subjects. But I suppose they will rather go to other islands for more secure protection. Mr. Walker is married well, and Mr. Jennings is about it. Our General designs to go for France in the Spring for his health; his distemper continuing."

LETTER CXXX.

To Colonel Hill, Deputy-Governor of St. Christopher's Island.

London, 20 January, 168⅘.

Sir.—I received your Honor's duplicate of the 18th of September, with an inclosed certificate, by the way of Ireland, by one Captain Martin. It came to my hands the second of this month. The original I had received not long before, *per* Captain Athy.

I am not unmindful of our private concerns, nor of the instructions you were pleased to give me touching the publick affairs of the island.

Sir William Stapleton, who is not yet recovered of his distemper, has been heard by the Lords of the Committee for Trade: to whom his Excellency offered several things relating to the islands in general under his government; and amongst other things, the Treaty of Neutrality, which was well received by some of the lords, and not by others.

I took this opportunity, with our General's consent, to get a petition drawn and directed to their Lordships, praying them to take that matter into their serious considerations, and by that or some other means to secure his Majesties subjects in those islands; which Alderman Lucy, Alderman Jefferys and Colonel Byar signed together with many other merchants and traders to those parts. And having gotten this petition thus signed, I took occasion the first day that their Lordships met to present it, which was on the 16th instant. But it was not read that day.

When I brought it to Mr. Blathwait, he sayd he wondered the merchants would trouble themselves now that Sir William Stapleton was here; and, for the Treaty of Neutrality, he sayd it was like a ball, that must be kept up to no purpose. But that men had gotten a notion of it, and would never lay it down, and that the French did but laugh at vs for it, and would never do it, and that they had long since refused it. I sayd the Count of Blanarque and the French governor in the island are and have been all along most desirous of it (as our Petition imports); but he replyed, it was no matter what the French do there, since the French here do but make sport at it. This was as neere as I can remember the words of Esquire Blathwait, who promised me nevertheless it should be read; but he added that if it were done, we should but deceive ourselves in expecting the French would keep it. I answered that the governors would be nevertheless watchful and upon their guard in tyme of danger; but that the people in the meantime would sit down more heartily, and the colony would be better peopled, and consequently in a better condition to make a defence, in case the French would break their faith, which I am apt to believe they might.

When I reflect upon the French proceeding in this Treaty of Neutrality, it seems to proceed from a politick desire to kill as it were with kindness; as I shall think, if they continue to deny the signing of it here. For after they affrighted or disturbed the English inhabitants with that considerable alarm in the year 1678, they proposed this amicable treaty; and as they have given us annual alarm ever since, so they have appeared most earnest for this unity—reflecting upon vs as the persons most backward in it, tho' in truth it was but themselves. But in the meantime, the English inhabitants were so amused with this treaty, that it was looked upon by them to be absolutely necessary to their safety. And when it appeared not feasible, they were so discouraged, that several of them withdrew to Carolina, to Jamaica and other places, not thinking their estates secure on St. Christopher's.

To revive the thoughts of this Treaty amongst the islands may be prejudicial, unless it take effect. When there is any probability of a war with France (which I do not perceive yet, unless at a great distance), it is a disadvantage to us that the vulgar inhabitants should have any thoughts of it before the tyme. For the very prospect of a war is capable to raise such apprehensions in them, as may make some of them desert the Island for fear of those dangers, which they would not be afraid to oppose upon a nearer approach.

The Royal African Company has made choice of Mr. Thomas Belchamber for their factor in the place of Mr. Robert Helmes.

On Thursday last, the Lord Delamere was tryed by twenty-eight of his peers in Westminster Hall, where scaffolds were erected for that purpose. The Lord Chancellor Jeffreys was made Lord High Steward; their Majesties, the Prince and Princess, with abundance of the nobility and gentry were spectators. There were eight or nine witnesses; but only one charged him positively with his treason. His name was Saxton. He swore that the Lord Delamere sent a servant for him, and that he came to his house in Cheshire, where the said lord, Sir Robert Cotton and Mr. Offley were together in a room; that they sent him of an errand into the west, to raise 10,000 men, and gave him 11 guinneys and five pounds to bear his charges. But when the prisoner came to make his defence, he endeavoured to prove Saxton an ill man. But he did not succeed well in that till he brought several very credible witnesses to prove, as they did most clearly, that not one of the three persons accused was that day which Saxton named at the sayd house: So far from it, that his Lordship was proved at that time to be in London; Mr. Offley went that day from Sir William Aston's (where he had been for eleven days) directly to his own house, and came not within some miles of the Lord Delamere's; and it was proved that Sir Robert Cotton did not stir out of London from the 10th of April till the beginning of August; and this consultation was pretended to be on the 4th of June. So the Lord Delamere was acquitted: and the other two will be discharged the next term; and a bill of indictment will be brought against Saxton for perjury.

The Lord Brandon Garrett* is reprieved; and so is Mr. Hambden, who pleaded guilty to his indictment of high treason, but denied having any knowledge of the design on the late King's person at the Rye. The Bishop of Durham is made Dean of the Royal Chapel at Whitehall, and one of the council in room of the Bishop of London, who is displaced; and the Bishop of Rochester is made cleark of the Closet.

People are much distracted with fears and jealousies, which make trading very dead. I am tould that Sir William Stapleton designs to take a journey into France before he returns to his government, which it is thought will not be till the latter end of the summer that is coming. There is a side-saddle in a box, marked Number CI, which

* Lord Gerard of Brandon.—J.C.J.

was put into my bill of store, and shipt with my goods, and is in my bill of loading. It belongeth to your lady, to whom I beg to tender my humble service, and with the like to Madam Windall, and the humble offer of the same to your Honor, I remain,

 Your Honor's most faithful and obedient servant,   CHRISTOPHER JEAFFRESON.

Postscript.—It is much discoursed that His Majesties Embasador in France has orders to demand the Principality of Orange for the Prince. Madam Sydley is with child and is now made Countess of Dorchester,* and has lodgings at Court. But newsletters are prohibited.

LETTER CXXXI.
To Captain Willett, a planter of St Christopher's Island. Dated from London, 24 January 168¾.

Thanking the captain for his trouble and

---

* The Countess of Dorchester's daughter by James II. the Lady Catherine Darnley, had by her marriage with the Earl of Anglesey an only daughter, Lady Catherine Annesley, who married William Phipps, only son of Sir Constantine Phipps, who was created Baron Mulgrave in the peerage of Ireland. Thus Stuart blood passed through Sir Charles Sedley's grand-daughter to the Lords Mulgrave and Marquises of Normanby.—J.C.J.

advice respecting the writer's West Indian property.

In reply to one of the captain's recommendations, the writer observes, "The good advice you were pleased to give me, touching the renting of my plantation, is what I have often ruminated upon as an expedient, to rid me of much vexation and trouble. But it is so difficult a matter to find an honest and sufficient tenant, that I cannot resolve upon it. For a poor tenant may soon be disabled, and a dishonest one will never be willing to comply with his lease. And I am sensible the law is more favourable to a tenant than an attourney. So that my case would be so much the worse. I should profit nothing by good years, and bear the whole loss of the bad. Therefore, if the way I have now taken does not succeed in some measures to my expectations, I think to sell is more advisable than to rent such an interest." In a manner, significant of his sense of quickly coming troubles in the mother-country, the writer adds, "*I do not know but St. Christopher's may be a good retirement and a better abode than this after a short tyme.* If so, I may chance to come, and thank you for all your kindness. If I should write the news of the town, I should amuse you with the representation of monstrous fears and jealousies. If there be reason for them, the event will soon show. And then you will probably hear it too soon, for ill news flies swift. It is good to hope the best, and in such hope I rest your faithful servant."

LETTER CXXXII.

To Mr. Sedgewick, the Writer's agent and steward in St. Christopher's Island—Dated from London, 22 January, 168$\frac{5}{6}$.

Containing instructions for the sale of a consignment of goods, sent out in the same ship as the letter; the goods being hats, linen, cloth, shoes, stockings and other articles of or material for raiment, as well as arms and gunpowder. Mr Sedgewick is required to store these goods and vend them "at the house," to which he must attract "cheapmen," *i.e.* customers, by underselling the regular store-keepers.

CHAPTER XIX.

WESTMINSTER AND THE WEST INDIES.

(28 January, 1685-6 to 2 March, 1685-6)

Sir William Stapleton's Health—The Queen's bitterness against the Countess of Dorchester—Lord Dartmouth—Changes and Rumours at Court—Chit-Chat—The King's Frugality—Sufferings of Voyagers—Homage rendered to the Countess of Dorchester—Legal Promotions—Lord Northampton's Disappointment—Duels and Duellists in High Life—The Duke of Grafton's Reappearance at Court—His Duel with Mr. Talbot.

LETTER CXXXIII.

To Captain James Phipps, a planter of St. Christopher's Island. Dated from London, 28 January, 168⅚.

Penned whilst the captain is making his way to the Leeward Islands, on his return from his brief holiday in Old England, this letter congratulates the voyager on his ascertained escape from the Isle of Wight, where he was wind-bound for a tedious time, and on his supposed restoration to the embraces of his gentle wife. The letter concludes with this gossip, "Sir William Stapleton designes to try if the French air will recover his health, and Ensign William Matthews accompanies him into France, and Lady Stapleton goes also; which voyage is intended in the month of March. Our brother Constantine and his lady and son are well. Madam Sydley is made Countess of Dorchester; but the Queen will not be satisfied, unless she depart the kingdom, or be stript of her allowance. The priests are very angry at her, for she is a kind of a Protestant, and there is a great feud between the flesh and the spirit. People discourse of great alterations in places at Court, as must be expected. The Lord Dartmouth has (it is sayd) leave to sell, and that the Earl of Dover is to succeed him. It is reported that the Duke of Ormond's place of Steward will be given to Earl Mulgrave, and that the Lord Walgrave will succeed him in his place of Chamberlaine. Discourses there are of a new Lord

Treasurer Powis, and a new Lord Chancellor Halifax, and a Vicar-General Jeffreys; but what credit to give the reports I know not. The Lord Arran, the Duke of Ormond's son, is dead; and the Lord Tyrconnell is Field Mareschall in Ireland, and his regiment is put in for by Tyrconnell and seven or eight other men of good interest."

[The letter-writer and John Evelyn concur in reporting the extreme displeasure of the principal Catholics at the favour and dignity lavished on Sir Charles Sedley's frail and fascinating daughter; but they differ as to the particular grounds of the disapproval. Whilst Evelyn says. " The Roman Catholics were also very angry; because they had so long valued the sanctity of their religion and proselytes," the present chronicler insinuates that the Catholics would have been less hurt had the King delighted to honour a gentlewoman of Catholic birth and education, whose antecedents were free from taint or suspicion of heresy.—J. C. J.]

LETTER CXXXIV.

To Mr. Sedgewick, the Writer's agent and steward in St. Christopher's Island. Dated from London, 29, 168¾.

A long letter about the accounts and prospects of the plantation, in which the writer takes a hopeful interest now that he has a steward on whom he can rely. With respect to Captain Rodeny's suggestion, that Mr. Sedgewick should accept a Commission in the Militia of the island, the writer (mindful how Mr. Thorn's military distinction and associates had stimulated his vanity and quickened his course to ruin) advises Mr. Sedgewick to decline the flattering invitation. "I am pleased," says the writer, "to hear Captain Rodeny is civil to you, but I consider those places and offices in the Militia are much more chargeable than honourable, and will draw you into more inconveniences than you are, perhaps, aware of. I would advise you to all frugality and good husbandry in all your proceedings, and in that respect remember England. We have before us a great example of frugality in our present King; and 'Regis ad exemplum totus componitur orbis.'"

LETTER CXXXV.

To ——, the Writer's "worthy friend" in St. Christopher's Island. Dated from London, 29 January, 168⅘.

After speaking of freights and cargoes of sugar, the writer observes to his worthy friend, " I hope you will receive a letter of an old date by Captain Winter, who has sailed from the Downes about two months, and has on board Sir James Russell, Captain Pogson, Captain Phipps, Mr. Lattee, Mr. Sympkin and two Ministers, Abraham Rezio, and several others, who have suffered incredible hardships and dangers, having been three or four times very near perishing on the rocks. And they do but half live on board. The Master's provisions and allowances are so bad, that Sir James (who, as I am informed, has a Commission for Lieutenant-General, until Sir William Stapleton retourns to the Islands), is so disheartened, that he has thoughts of quitting the ship, and seeking for a new passage at

Bristol:—Winter being now sayd to be at Plymouth, where his ship, it seemes, struck upon the rocks in going in. Our General designed in March to try the French air for his health; and Ensign William Matthews will accompany him. We had a strong report that our King, in the right of the Prince of Orange, had ordered his Embassador at Paris to demand the Principality of Orange. But it is contradicted; and we have so many false reports, that it is imprudent, as well as dangerous, to write any news. But Madam Sydley is made Countess of Dorchester, at which the Queen took such distaiste, that the Countess was ordered to remove, as I hear, from Court and kingdom. But to the latter, she suspends her obedience. Several persons of quality went to congratulate her on her new honor, which likewise was taken notice of by her Majestie."

[Speaking of the Queen's natural indignation at the exaltation of Charles Sedley's daughter, John Evelyn says:—" 19 Jan. 1686. Passed the Privy Seal, amongst others, the creation of Mrs. Sedley (concubine to ———) Countess of Dorchester, which the Queen took very grievously, so as for two dinners, standing near her, I observed she hardly eat one morsel, nor spoke one word to the King, or to any about her, though at other times she used to be extremely pleasant, full of discourse and good humour."—J. C. J.]

LETTER CXXXVI.

To Major Crispe, a planter of St. Christopher's Island. Dated from London, 30 January, 168¾.

Opening with a reference to the dangers and distresses encountered by Sir James Russell, Captain Phipps, and the other gentlemen of the island, who, starting for their voyage back to the West Indies on 10 Nov. last, have been so retarded and driven about by adverse winds, that they have made no greater way than Plymouth, where they are now resting, till their ship can be repaired and re-victualled. " The Treaty of Neutrality," the writer says at the end of his letter, " is now in agitation, but Mr.

Blathwait says the French have positively rejected it, and will never do it. Sir William Stapleton is going in March with his Lady and Ensign William Matthews to France, and he designs to retourn to his government before the hurricane season, as he tells me; and I hear Sir James Russell has a commission for the Lieutenant-General in his absence. I do not see any probability of a war this summer with any of our neighbours; and people are quiet at home. The law has its due course, and the religion established is freely professed, according to his Majestie's gracious declaration. There has been some alteration of officers at Court, as well as in the new army, and several discoursed of. Such chainges we may expect, and the consequences of them."

LETTER CXXXVII.

Ta Colonel Hill, Deputy-Governor of St. Christopher's Island.

London, 2 March, 168$\frac{5}{6}$.

Honoured Sir.—Perceiving that the Royal African Company had not of late ordered any ship to supply the Leeward Islands with negroes, and that one ship, hired for St. Christopher's, had, on the petition of the owners, her voyage altered, so that at this tyme there is no ship upon the coast, nor any provision made to supply your Island, or any other under our General's government, I thought it very necessary to put the Company in mind of your letter to them; which I did last Thursday, and met with a cold reception from the Committee. Sir Benjamin Bathurst, the Deputy-Governor, answered me that the Company had received great losses by that trade, and that your Island was much indebted to them, that they did send supplys to Nevis, and that St. Christopher's, which was a very small colony, might supply themselves from thence, if they pleased; but that if any persons would purchase a ship's loading of them for St Christophers's, they would fournish them, and give good tyme for the payment of the money. I replyed that to my knowledge St. Christopher's made as good payments as any of the islands, and that it was very considerable, and capable to take off 900 or a thousand negroes in a year's tyme; but for purchasing negroes here I could say little, there being fow of that island provided with such stocks in England as to make that purchase. Considering we had no other way or means to fournish ourselves with slaves, our dependency was upon them, that they would send us supplies upon the same terms as they did to the other islands.

But all that I could gain from them at present was that they would write to your Honor about it, in answer to your letter to them. But Mr. Herron, the secretary, told me since that the matter was debated after I was withdrawn, and that it is resolved a ship should be forthwith dispatched for the supply of St. Christopher's and Nevis only. After which they shall be solicited for more, for I find it a very troublesome and difficult matter to get servants, and now the Dartmouth is in your neighbourhood, it will be hard for interlopers to do their business, so that I know not how we shall procure hands to carry on our works.

I perceive my attourneys are so indulgent to Ensign Thorn, that he is left to his own liberty to comply when and how he pleaseth with the award of the commissioners; which at his first demand they are ready to perform on my part, before they receive my objections to his unjust account, by which I suffer severely.

I hope your Honor will do me right, as to my dividend of the produce of the malefactors I sent. I have been long out of my money, which I did not design, for the use of my plantation. I am still desirous that our sugars should be shipped home togeather; that the freight and charges being equal on every man's part, the clear produce here might be justly and equally divided, as was at first agreed; and, if not so, that I may have my share. And I think I ought to be advanced now, as much as I have hitherto been behind in receipts. Mr. Vickers writes me word he had designed to ship me some sugars, but that your Honor's mind was altered, and that you would receive as much for yourself and me as he had taken for himself, and then I should have my share. I should accept it as a favour if you would be pleased to order it any-way, for it would be welcome to me, now that I have no returns from my plantation, and am continually laying out moneys for the supplying it with servants and necessaries.

Sir Thomas Jenner is made a Baron of the Exchequer, and Sir John Holt is now Recorder of London. The Parliament in Scotland will sit the next moneth, the Lord Murray is going Commissioner. The Lord Mulgrave, now Lord Chamberlain, is about to be married to the Lady Conway, of whom the Lord of Northampton thought himself secure, but was abused in it by Mr. Seymour, who is much blamed; but it is sayd he gets money by it. His Majestie has been very angry at a duel lately fought between Sir Charles Compton's son and Mr. Seymour's second or third son. They were both wounded, and will be prosecuted as duellists. The Duke of Grafton is at Court again; the killing of the Earl of Shrewsbury's brother was what Mr. Talbot drew upon himself by giving great provocations, and at last a challenge. I wish all health and happiness to your Honor, to your Ladyship and to Mrs. Windall, to whom I present my most humble service, remaining as ever,

Sir, Your Honor's most obedient humble servant,

CHRISTOPHER JEAFFRESON.

CHAPTER XX.

THE LATEST NEWS.

(2 March 1685-6 to 4 June, 1686.)

The Parson of Woppenham—Legal Rumours—Illness of the French King—French Protestants—Religious Persecution in Piedmont—The Camp on Hounslow Heath—French Designs on the Plate Fleet—Official changes in Ireland—Religious Animosities in London—Storms at Sea—Constantine Phipps settled at Fulham—An unsettled Account—Distress of the French Refugees—Charitable Relief of the Sufferers—The Fall of the Bull Inn.

LETTER CXXXVIII.

To Mr. Sedgewick, the Writer's agent and steward in St. Christopher's Island. Dated from London, 2 March, 168$\frac{5}{6}$.

Containing orders about the plantations, and some pieces of domestic news. Mrs. Sedgewick, the steward's mother, is dead; and Mr. Hart, the parson of Woppenham, has been murdered by a butcher, who in a frenzy of jealousy and vengeance "knocked out the brains" of his wife's paramour. "I have sent you," says the writer, "two servants, a man and a woman, with a copy of their indentures. The man, Hugh Newton for four years and nine months, is, as I am informed, a very honest young man, not bred to much labour, but he writes indifferent well, and can do any easy work, and will prove, I hope, a profitable servant, The woman for five years, is, as I am told, a good needle-woman, can make or mend negroes' or servants' cloathes. As you have two of them, you may keep the best in the house, and turn the other to grass; for none of my people must be idle. A sugar-work affords employment for all sorts of people. I wish you good luck with them. I have spent some money to procure more men, and have failed in my enterprise."

LETTER CXXXIX.

To Colonel Hill, Deputy-Governor of St. Christopher's Island.

No date.

Sir.—I have received your Honor's letter by Captain Chant, the day that I came to town, having been in Suffolk and Cambridgeshire, which prevented my writing by Captain Nicolls, who went down to Gravesend the morrow after my coming to London. So that I had only time to give my service to your Honor in a short epistle to Mr. Sedgewick, which I scribbled over at a coffee-house, where Captain Nicolls was.

The certificate is such as was required or vs here to clear our bonds, which made me request it. Thus it happened I gave you a needless trouble; for when Mr. Recorder understood that we designed to trouble him no more with the Order of Council, I easily prevailed with him, with the former certificate, to cancel our bond, which I was earnest with him to do, before he was removed; least he should have left vs in bonds. He is made one of the Barons of the Exchequer, and Mr. Holt, now Sir John Holt, is Recorder of London. The Lord Chief Justice Jones, Mr. Justice Levins, Sir Job Charleton, the Lord Chief Baron Montague, and some other judges have their quietus, and new judges are put in their places. Sir — Benningfield is Lord Chief Justice of the Common Pleas. Sir Edward Atkens is Lord Chief Baron, and several serjeants were called this term.

The Duke of Albemarle is said to be going Governor of Jamaica ; and if we may credit reports, he is to bear the character of Vice-Roy of all his Majesties Dominions in America, which I doubt ; and I believe, if such a thing be, it will signifie no more but a tytle of honor.

Your Honor is pleased to make mention in your letter of the malefactors, and what is due to me on that accompt, on which subject I have been so large in my other letters, that I need not trouble your Honor at this tyme about it. For I rely upon your good justice in the case, who, I doubt not, will see that I have right done me in it. And for the charge that we were at concerning those unsold, I should think the labour of those that are well should sufficiently recompense the charge of the sick. But, to put an end to that difference, I should think it advisable to divide those unsold equally amongst vs concerned, that we may as equally share the profit as we do the charge of the servants. For it is hard that one plantation should be the hospital for all the distressed. I hope that before this can arrive, all the debts on this score will be collected, excepting such as are desperate.

I have heard from Sir William Stapleton since he went for France. The French King is still dangerously ill, and it is feared is past recovery; but he may linger out a painful and uneasy life for some tyme. The persecution of the Protestants continues in that country in a most cruel manner, and there is a report of a massacre in Piedmont, in the Duke of Savoy's territories, in which eight or ten thousand were butchered. But of this we have not yet any certainty as to the particulars. In the meantyme, thanks be to God, we enjoy the free exercise of our religion, as by law established. And it is certainly the interest of every Protestant, as well as his duty, to be loyal and obedient both to God and the King.

Here are great preparations making for the campaign; the army being ordered to encamp very suddenly on Hounslow Heath, both horse and foot. Every commission-officer has his tent, which is a very great charge to the officers. This last year has been an unprofitable year for the officers. I think the Horse Guards will not encamp.

His Majestie has been pleased to grant a brief for the relief of such French Protestants as have escaped hither from the cruel persecution; and the contributions are very liberal.

The French Fleet lies now before Cales. It is feared it has a designe upon the Plate Fleet, in which the Dutch and English merchants are much concerned.

Sir, I beg to tender my humble service to your lady and sisters, and to Mrs. Windall, and to beg that you would be pleased to accept the same yourself from,

    Sir, Your Honor's most humble obedient servant,

        CHRISTOPHER JEAFFRESON.

P.S.—The Treaty of Neutrality has been negotiated here by one Monsieur Bonrepos, Intendant de la Marine en France, who is returned thither; and tho' his proceedings are kept very private, I am informed it is concluded on, but not ratified or signed, till which tyme I am told it will be kept private at the Plantation Office. They only say it is likely to be done, when Sir William Stapleton returnes; who, I hear, is much indisposed with his distemper and the fatigue of his journey into France, where it is thought he will make but a short stay, if he does not find an amendment of his health.

LETTER CXL.

To Mr. Sedgewick, the Writer's agent and steward in St. Christopher's Island. Dated from London, 8 May, 1686.

Respecting the affairs of the plantation, and more particularly about the policy of planting Balcony Hill with canes, when so much land of superior quality lies nearer the sugar-work. "I have," the writer observes, "sent your saddle and furniture you writ for by Captain Came. You may cut the pistols I gave you, or wear them as they are, till we are in a better capacity to follow the modes. As I would not oppose, so I do not rejoyce in the office which Captain Rodeny is so civil as to offer you; which is a bait to draw you to an unnecessary expense, as well as to neglect of affaires. I will be so free with you, as to tell you that it is not for your interest. For if you do not live closely and retiredly, especially at first, the plantation will not answer your expectations nor mine. The hearkening to the allurements of company abroad, and intrusting too much to servants at home, is what I would caution you of, as it was the path that led Ensign Thorn to the ruin of my interest if not of his own."

LETTER CXLI.

To Captain James Phipps, a planter in St. Christopher's Island.

London, 3 May, 1686.

Dear Brother .... Both here and in Ireland are great alterations of judges and officers. Yet the Catholick cause advances but slowly. In short I will tell you a truth, which a reverend divine spoke seasonable the last Sunday:—" Our adversaries would fain catch something else, and they know there is no better fishing than in troubled waters. To prevent this hellish design, let vs study to be quiet, and learn to know it is our interest, as well as our duty, to be so." In Mincing Lane, in London, the Romanists would needs have a room to say mass in, which was allowed; and every Sunday since the chapel was opened, some or other persons have been clapt vp and secured, to prevent the disturbing them, who, it is sayd, are now about to remove those devotions to a more convenient place.

This week a book was burned by the hand of the common hangman, being a relation of the cruel persecutions of the Protestants in France, which the Romanists deny. We see men fly from their country by stealth, from their estates and relations, to live on the charity of strangers, and yet we must not believe in a persecution.

[The copy of this letter is imperfect; a note in the writer's hand observing, "This letter was *finished* with news, and sent by Captain Chant the 10th of May, 1686." —J. C. J.]

LETTER CXLII.

To Mr. Sedgewick, the Writer's agent and steward in St. Christopher's Island. Dated from London, 4 June, 1686.

Discussing at great length the affairs of the plantations.

"It pleases me," says the writer, "to hear that your garden thrives so well, and that you take a delight in it, which makes me promesse myself you will make a good planter, and that you will in tyme take pleasure in the great garden, I mean the plantation, when you see it full of canes. A kitchen-garden, I know, is very necessary and useful for you. I fear flowers will not do so well there, except such as you see in your neighbours' gardens; but I desire that by your next you would inform me what flower-seeds you would have me send you. . . . I have herewith sent you Gervase Markham's 'Whole Art of Husbandry,' and Sir William Hughs his 'American Physician,' which are the two books you writ for. The first I had by me, and the other I bought, and payd as much for it, tho' a second-hand book, as if it were new, because it is out of print and hard to come by. . . . The book called · The Schoole of Vertue' is for Hugh Newton."

LETTER CXLIII.

To Captain James Phipps, a planter in St. Christopher's Island.

London, 4 June, 1686.

Dear Brother.—I am heartily glad to hear that you are arrived safe and in good health at St. Christopher's, after your long and perilous voyage, which made me and all your friends here impatient of the tyme till Captain Webster dispersed our doubts by the good news of your well-being.

My brother and sister Lewis, who are now both in town, and give their services to you, went with me one day the last week to see our brother Constantine and his lady at Fulham, where they intend to spend most part of the summer. Only he must attend his occasions. We were very merry and drank your good health in a glass of very good wine. I have seen him since, and imparted to him the good news I had then received from St. Christopher's. Your pretty daughter and all your friends in this clymate are well. I know at your first arrival you must be full of business, as well as of the company of your friends, who will flock to congratulate you on your safe arrival and great deliverance. But when leisure and a cessation of visits will give you leave, I beg your favour of a few lines to say how you bore the winter. I am afraid you will not be easily induced to look northward this long tyme again, for that you met with such a bad winter. It will make the summer the more pleasant to you, where I hope you will meet with such good seasons as will make amends for the bad weather you had on our coast. Our General is still in France, and his distemper continues, which I am sorry for.

 I am your faithful servant and most affectionate brother,

CHRISTOPHER JEAFFRESON.

LETTER CXLIV.

To Mr. Vickers, a planter of St. Christopher's Island. Dated from London, 4 June, 1686.

Condoling with Mr. Vickers on the loss he has sustained in the capture of a ship off the "coast of Guinea."

Touching on London news, the writer says; "The chief discourse of the town at present is of the army, encamped on Hounslow Heath, where the poor men are like to suffer much by the cold and extreame wet weather, which is not suitable to the time of the year. But, however their bodies fare, there is great care taken for their souls. There are Priests and Levites. Mass for one party, and Common Prayer for another. Our friend Mr. Parkhurst is made chaplain to the Duke of Somerset and to one of his regiments Our clergymen do their duties admirably well. The Romanists are foiled in the paper engagements. Our arguments are too strong for them; and sometymes in our discourse we ramble from this religious, ill-victualled camp to poor Scotland, where the parliament is now sitting; and, if gold does not work upon them more than fair promises have done, they will not part with their old Mumpsimus for ere a new Sumpsimus in Christendom. An old satyre said they had once sold their King, but 'twas hoped they would not sell their G—. They seem loath to take away the Test. A few days now will show what will be done in it. Here are dayly discourses of more alterations amongst the Judges, which are expected. The Bull Inn in the Strand fell suddainely down, one morning lately, about six of the clock, and killed ten or twelve people who layd there that night. The Parliament here is prorogued to the 22nd of November."

CHAPTER XXI.

TATTLE OF THE CLIQUES.

(4 *June*, 1686 *to* 8 *September*, 1686.)

The Court at Windsor—Prorogation of Parliament—Sale of White Servants—Gifts to Colonial Governors—The Duke of Albemarle, Governor of Jamaica—Sir Edmund Andrews—The King's Treatment of the Navy—The New Ecclesiastical Commission—A Duel at Epsom—The New Privy Councillors—Sir William Stapleton's Death—Lady Stapleton's Troubles—Token Drinking at the Exchange Tavern—Proceedings against the Bishop of London—The Siege of Buda—Siege of Hamburgh by the Danes.

LETTER CXLV.

To Colonel Hill, Deputy-Governor of St. Christopher's Island.

London, 4 June, 1686.

Sir.—By Captain Webster I received a letter from your Honor, dated March the 22nd. It came but few days since to my hands; and I am glad I have so soon met with an opportunity to retourne my thanks for the favour.

My sister, who with my brother Lewis is now in town at their old house in Channell Row, gives her service to your Honor, and your Lady and Madam Windall, with thanks for your kind remembrance of them. They are come to take leave of the town for a year or two, designing to retourn into the country about July next. They have a fine being in Glamorganshire. But it is so far, and the ways so bad thither, it is not convenient to come often to town. But, when they do come, they mean to make some considerable stay here, as I hope they will.

I thank your Honor that you are pleased to be mindful of what is due to me on accompt of the malefactors. My profits on that account, though at the best but small, will be made much less for the long want of the money layd out upon it. I have insisted so much on that subject in former letters, that it is needless to add more words at this tyme; but I shall wait your Honors pleasure in it; who, I depend upon it, will take some course, that I may be satisfied in this most reasonable demand, seeing it lyes wholly in your power to put an equitable period to this now old accompt, as I may modestly call it; who had the first and most of the trouble, and am like to have the last if not the least share of the profit, which with fruitless expectations I have long hoped for.

Your Honor's proceedings in giving protection to the poor distressed French Protestants is praiseworthy; and I think is not liable to the blame of any Christian, except the most Christian King. It is no more than what is done here. His Majestie has granted them a brief; and very great collections have been made in and about the City. Few gentlemen give less than a guinea, some give two and some three, and so to a hundred. Their condition is very deplorable, though some who can outface the light of the sun, stick not to deny or palliate the cruelties and inhumanities, used by the dragoons, who are a new kind of missionary to make conversions and settle religion. There are great numbers who, unable to indure the horrid severities of this persecution, have resigned their consciences to receive such impressions as these Apostolical Dragoons had orders to stamp on them; and have been so far imposed on, as to give it under their hands, that what they did was voluntary. Though now, I am told, many of these, labouring under the sad terrors of a troubled conscience for what they had done, renounce their own act, and would gladly suffer death, to end the miseries of a tired and wearisome life.

If our arms should not be open to those, who have so freely abandoned their native country, their friends, relations and estates, and all that was dear to them in this world, for the alone sake of God and the true and pure religion, we should share with the cruel persecutors in the want of Christian charity. Pardon, dear sir, this freedom. As you are pleased to give me an accompt of what you have done in this case, I take the liberty to declare my opinion, that in so doing you have served your King and your Country and your God.

It is in effect the fulfilling of the true intent of that very law which, in the literal sense, seems to forbid it. For as I was assistant at the making of that act, I can say it was made in order to the peopling his Majestie's colony on St. Christopher's Island with English subjects, and to lay some hardships on such as, having English plantations amongst vs, had actually layd down their arms, and declared that they, on no occasions, would bear arms against their native Prince. Now these French Protestants, being become obnoxious to the penalties of their country's laws, whenever taken, are necessitated to be faithful to those amongst whom they find safety and refuge. And so, as I sayd, his Majestie's colony is by the protection of these men (who in one generation will become perfect Englishmen in interest, religion, and language), peopled and strengthened by so many new subjects; who in all probability will be as faithful to his Majestie as his own natural subjects. This is my opinion in which I hope I am not deceived.

The new army is encamped upon Hounslow Heath; that is, the foot. The horse does not encamp till the latter end of this month. The season has been extraordinary cold and wet for the tyme of the year, and that has occasioned some sickness. But that is not the only complaynt. The providers made such excessive profits by the sutlers, that they were forced to pinch it out of the poor soldiers' bellies. But his Majestie has given orders for the rectifying that abuse. There is as much religion in this camp as ever was in any I have heard of. In one tent is masse, in another common prayer; in one tent preaching, in another praying to the saints; here the beads, there the bible; and such a wonderful care of souls as if no ennemy but the Devil were near them. These diversities of doctrines must needs divide men's opinions. Every sentinel will be able to dispute the point; and men, thus provided with arms and arguments, may, for aught I know, conquer the Turks and all the world, when they please. For what was before shared between the gown-men and the sword-men will be possibly found in one man.

The Bull Inn, near the new Exchainge, one night last month, about six of the clock, fell flat to the ground, and killed and buried some sixteen persons, of whom ten or twelve dyed.

Sir William Stapleton continues in France, and is still afflicted with his old distemper.

Ensign Matthews has buried his youngest son. He had the good luck to continue in town this wet weather.

Mr. Baxter has been dangerously ill of a fever, and is not yet recovered. All the rest of your friends are well. The Court is at Windsor. The Parliament is prorogued to the 22nd of November. In Scotland the Parliament sits; and they have many eyes upon them, expecting what they will do, in taking away or confirming the law, for the test is sayd to be the matter in debate. In Ireland there are many changes of judges and officers. The Lord Tyrconnell is gone over thither.

Sir, Your Honor's most obedient humble servant.

CHRISTOPHER JEAFFRESON.

LETTER CXLVI.

To Mr. Sedgewick, the Writer's agent and steward in St. Christopher's Island. Dated from London, 3 August, 1686.

A long letter of instructions for the conduct of the plantations, and shipment of produce. In a passage, which exhibits with singular vividness the complete dependence of inferior bond-servants on the will of their employers in the West Indies, the writer forbids his steward to sell (*i. e.* hire out) his white servants (not being malefactors) without their consent. "I have," he says, "passed my word to the maid-servant I sent last, that she should not be sold; nor would I have you dispose of any white servants of mine; for it was never my intention to send any excepting goal-birds on that accompt. If you have the convenience of hiring her out for a year or two with her consent till the other is free, she will be the more fit to look after the family, when the other is gone. If nobody will hire her, the worst of the two must do the servile work. She must not be sold, because of my promise, which I value much." A postscript to the epistle announces that the writer has just received the news of Sir William Stapleton's death at Paris.

LETTER CXLVII.

To Colonel Hill, Deputy-Governor of St. Christopher's Island.

[*Note.*—The writer will not fail to observe that the earlier part of this letter was penned before the writer had received intelligence of Sir William Stapleton's death, which was followed quickly by his burial in Paris—J. C. J.]

London, 3 August, 1686.

Sir.—Your Honor's commands by Captain Hare I have received; which shall be obeyed so soon as Sir William Stapleton retournes from France, where he yet continues for his health, being in a fair way for recovery.

I cannot see why the Assembly should be so scrupulous in making gifts to their governors, unless there were a confirmation of that order which was made in the late King's tyme; which I think is not confirmed by his now Majestie. This is my opinion in which I may err; but it is grounded on this, that the Justices of the Peace here refused to bind servants for the plantations, according to the order, made by his late Majestie in Council, December the 13th, 1682, but looked upon it that it dyed with the King. And his now Majestie has renewed that order; and there are particular offices erected for it in London and the seaport towns. If there be any danger in it; certainly those, to whose advantage such a gift is made, should be very careful to inquire if the hazard of the inconvenience did not outweigh the profit attending it, before they would accept it.

The Treaty of Neutrality, (or of trade and commerce, as I hear it will be called) is still doing, Mr. Blathwait tould me not long since. And he says the Acts and everything else shall be ready against the General goes. His Majestie's will is to nominate all the Gentlemen of his Council for every island; and some new instructions there will be, but all affairs are carried on with extraordinary secresy.

I cannot hear of any Governor nominated for Barbadoes. The Duke of Albemarle holds yet his resolution of accepting the government of Jamaica (where we hear that runaway negroes are very troublesome). Sir Edmund Andrews is going out as Governor of New England, and will embarque very suddainely. He tould me the King had promised him some commanded men.

His Majestie had lately before him the Commanders of his navy, and made a very handsome speech to them; the scope of which was (as I am informed) to let them know how well he was acquainted with several misdemeanours, too frequent amongst them; that he would pardon all that is past but nothing hereafter of that kind; and that he was sensible their allowance was too small, and therefore had given order their tables should be doubled; which order being read, he bade them repayre to their respective commands.

There are seven Commissioners appointed to inspect Ecclesiastical affairs. What their proceedings will be tyme must shew. The persons nominated are the Archbishop of Canterbury, the Bishop of Durham, and the Bishop of Rochester, for the tyme being; the four laymen are the Lord Chancellor, the Lord Treasurer, the Lord President, and the Lord Chief Justice, for the tyme being. And Mr. Bridgman is register to them.

Eleven of the twelve judges have given their opinions that his Majestie may dispense with the Test.

Since the Lord Tyrconnell went over into Ireland, where he is commander-in-chief of all military affairs, there have been great changes in that army. A great number of officers have been displaced, and many souldiers.

The camp here at Hounslow is very glorious. His Majestie is there almost every day. There is great concourse to it, and great feasting at it; often exercising, and much powder burnt. Captain Freeman has layd down his commission, as some other officers did before—the company or the expense of which, I perceive, many are now weary of. They must have double tables too, or it won't hold out, and double pay.

The Lord Powis, the Lord Arundel of Warder, the Lord Bellasis, and the Lord of Dover, are all four sworn of his Majestie's Council.

Captain Freeman has had the misfortune lately to wound a gentleman of his own name in a duel, which happened upon a slight occasion at Epsom, as they were in company. The Captain and his second are wounded likewise; but are retired till a pardon is procured, for Mr. Freeman of Surrey is dead. I am sorry that I have yet more and worse ill news to write you. I just now received a letter, which brings me the sad intelligence of the death of our General, Sir William Stapleton. He dyed and was buried at Paris, to the great loss and grief of all under his government. Mr. Martin had a letter this day from the Lady Stapleton, who is still in France, and certainly in great grief.

I cannot give your Honor a positive answer to the question concerning my retourn to the Indies, which depends so much upon the uncertain events of my affairs, that I cannot take any resolution in it. Our General not long before he went to France put the same question to me, and partly for the same reason, that makes you now propose it. I was not to be relyed upon, by reason of the uncertainty of my business, here as well as there. But now I have no more to pretend on that score; for my commissions die with him that gave them.

Sir, you may perceive this letter was written at several tymes, by the different advices it gives, which were according to Mr. Martin's letters from France. Probably there was some appearance of an amendment before his end, as is usual in such cases. I leave the rest to my good friend Mr. Duport, who hath promised to oblige me in conveighing this with my humble service to your Honor, to your Lady, your sister and Mrs. Windall, &c., &c.

CHRISTOPHER JEAFFRESON.

LETTER CXLVIII.

To Major Crispe, a planter in St. Christopher's Island.

[*Note.*—Another of the letters touching the usage of token-drinking and token-feasts. —J. C. J.|

London, 8 September, 1686.

Having lately participated in the noble token, which you sent by Mr. Davis, I am obliged to retourn my thanks for that favour. Wednesday last we met Mr. Davis, who being about to go into his own country in Wales, where he intends to settle, could not depart with a safe conscience, till he had discharged the trust you imposed on him. He spoke to Mr. Cary, Mr. Wrayford, and one or two more, and left a note at my lodgings, that I might meet him at the Exchange, whence we went to the sayd tavern, and were merry at your charge.

And, it being a large token, we employed double means to consume it—by eating as well as by drinking—least that by too much of the latter, we should have forgotten ourselves under pretence of remembering our friends.

Since the departure of your neighbour, Mr. Duport, the great discourse of the town has been concerning the proceedings of the Lords Commissioners for Ecclesiastical affairs against the Bishop of London, for not suspending Dr. Sharpe, as by his Majesties letters he had been commanded. He made a good and ingenious defence, showing that he had obeyed the sayd command, as far as he was advised he could by law; and that the sayd Doctor had not since preached in his diocese. Notwithstanding, on Monday last, the Lords proceeded to a definitive sentence, and suspended him from his office during the King's pleasure.

We have been likewise very much concerned about the siege of Buda. Great wagers and odds have been layd on both sides, and money lost on both sides; for, tho' it be at last taken, some, who were over-forward in their reckoning, payd for their presumption, who knew nothing but by chimera. The siege of Hamburgh by the Danes is of more immediate consequence to our merchants, who are like to suffer much by the frequent fires caused by the bombs which are shot into the city. But the taking of Buda is of great importance to Christendom. I will only beg leave to make the tender of my service to your lady and the young ladies, your daughters, and beg that you would accept the same yourself from him that is, Sir,

Your most faithful servant,
CHRISTOPHER JEAFFRESON.

Mr. Nicholas Crispe and his lady are well. She was brought to bed about a month since of a brave boy.

CHAPTER XXII.

THE LAST LETTERS OF THE FOURTH YEAR IN LONDON.

(8 *September*, 1686, *to* 16 *September* 1686.)

A Royal Progress—Trial of the Bishop of London by the Ecclesiastical Commissioners—Dr. Sharp, Rector of St. Giles's in the Fields—**Arguments of Counsel and the Sentence**—Refusal of the Bantam Claims—Lady Stapleton and the French Priests—Constantine Phipps on the Welsh Circuit—Health-Drinking at Cambridge Assizes—Capture of Buda—Mrs. Sarah Gordon of Goodman's Fields—Advice to Lieutenant Munday—Sir Nathaniel Johnson's Preparations for a Voyage to the Leeward Islands.

LETTER CXLIX.

To Colonel Hill, Deputy-Governor of St. Christopher's Island.

London, 8 September, 1686.

Since the departure of Mr. Duport, by whom I writ to your Honor, I have little more to impart, but what he could inform you of.

Before he got clear of the Downs, it was known that Sir Nathaniel Johnson was appointed to succeed Sir William Stapleton in his government. He is preparing for his voyage; but I presume he will not depart hence these two or three months. I am not known to him as yet, but was the other day to wait on your sister, Madam Farmer, to advise with her about making application to your friends, about matters that may happen by this change, which I shall endeavour to serve you in, as soon as the Court retourns hither.

His Majestie has been on a progress into the west. He was at Bristol, Bridgewater, Wilton, Southampton, Portsmouth, &c., and came to Windsor last Tuesday. The same day the Bishop of London appeared before the Ecclesiastical Commissioners: it being the day appointed for him to give in his answer to the question, why he did not suspend Dr. Sharpe according to his Majestie's command? The Bishop offered at first to plead to the * * to speak to it; but the Lord Chancellor told him he would neither hear him nor any of council in the matter; they being well satisfied with their Commission and the authority that gave it. Then the Bishop delivered in his answer in writing, and spake very handsomely with much submission. He sayd, he proceeded in this matter with the advice of such as were learned in the laws, who informed him that suspension was a legal act, in which he was to proceed judicially and not otherwise. Upon which he writ back to the King to acquaint his Majestie with it, and how that he was ready to proceed against the Doctor in that manner, if his Majestie thought fit, and so expected to receive his Majesties farther commands. But that, in the meantyme, he sent for Dr. Sharpe, and having acquainted him of his Majestie's displeasure and the occasion of it, shewed him the King's letter, and moreover advised him not to preach till farther order; and that accordingly he had not preached since then in his Diocese. And he desired that the Council, by whom he had been thus advised, might be heard to give their reasons before their Lordships, which was granted: and four Doctors in Civil Law pleaded his cause, viz: Dr. Hodges, Dr. Oldish, Dr. Newton and Dr. Price. The main scope of their argument was to prove that the Bishop could by no law suspend a Minister before he was heard; that suspension was the execution of a sentence in law of nature and the law of nations; and that therefore it could not be understood that his Majestie intended a suspension *ab officio*, but only a silencing of him, to which the Bishop had obeyed. The Bishop sayd, that if in form or method he had failed in his obedience to the royal command, he was heartily sorry for it, begged his Majestie's pardon, and was ready to make what reparation his Majestie should require. He desired their Lords would put the most favourable construction upon what he sayd, seeing he spoke *ex tempore*. The Court adjourned to Monday the 6 of September, and on the sayd day they met accordingly, and after a long deliberation, the Bishop was called in, and the sentence was read, of which I will give you the words as near as I can remember them. That whereas the sayd Bishop had been convened before that Court, and had been fully heard, as to the matter wherewith he was charged—the Commissioners had thought fit to proceed to a definitive sentence : and the sayd Bishop of London, for his disobedience and other his disrespect to his Majestie's command, should be suspended ; and that he was by them declared suspended from his office during the King's pleasure, and that he should not presume to officiate in the same upon pain of being totally deprived. These, as near as I can remember, are the words, or sum of the sentence, which I heard pronounced by Mr. Bridgeman, the Secretary to the Lords Commissioners. The Bishop has behaved himself so well in this affair, with such temper and prudence, that he is highly applauded for it; and I have great hopes that, upon his submission, he will be received again into his Majestie's favour and be restored. But there are many of a contrary opinion. This new Commission having taken up the greatest part of the discourse of the town, I have been the larger in the account of this first proceeding upon it, which is very remarquable. The other part of the discourse of the town has been concerning the siege of Buda, the most famous siege that haith happened in the memory of man, and of great consequence to both empires. The Christians, after having encountered a very stout resistance, made themselves masters of that important place, almost in view of a great army, led by the Grand Vizier to the relief of it. Hamburgh is now invested by the Danes, who do great damage to the town, with their bombs, at which our merchants are not a little concerned. The inclosed, from Mr. Farmer, I received this morning. I pray give my service to your Lady and to Madam Windall, and to your sister.

Your Honor's most faithful humble servant,
CHRISTOPHER JEAFFRESON.

Postscript.—The Hollander does not give that satisfaction as was expected and demanded for the injuries done our merchants at Bantam. The consequences of which may be expected. I am told the King has dispensed with the order, prohibiting presents to the Governor of Barbadoes.

LETTER CL.

To Captain James Phipps, a planter in St. Christopher's Island.

London, 8 September, 1686.

By my last I gave you the sad news of Sir William Stapleton's death, whose lady is now at Camberwell with Lady Marsh. The French priests were very unkind to her, and still detain her sons out of some religious pretence, with no small addition to the grief of her ladyship, who is deprived at once of a husband and her sons. The General was so sensible before he died of the designs of some, that he had entrusted with the execution of his will, that it much discomposed him in his extremity, and he endeavoured to make some alterations, and would have done more, if death had not prevented him.

The treaty of Neutrality is so far perfected, that it is supposed there will be nothing altered of what is now agreed on; but it is not yet signed, though there is no doubt but it will be; and when it is, I shall know it possibly before it comes to the Plantation Office.

I presume it is no news to you, that there are several persons here who make it their business to make remarks upon the sermons of our ministers, and to make report, true or false, of what they pretend to have heard; and that Dr. Sharpe, rector of St. Giles's-in-the-Fields, an eminent preacher, was accused to have preached sedition, upon which the Lord Sunderland, by the command of his Majestie writ a letter to the Bishop of London, ordering him to suspend the doctor for the said offence. . . . . . .

* * * * *

Our brother Constantine is gone the Welsh Circuit. The rest of your friends here are well. I pray, give my service to the ministers and all our friends. I drank Mr. Parris's and Mr. Chid's health last Cambridge assizes.

Your affectionate brother and humble servant.

CHRISTOPHER JEAFFRESON.

LETTER CLI.

To Mr. Sedgewick, the Writer's agent and steward in St. Christopher's Island.

London, 8 September, 1686.

Mr. Duport, who embarqued in Captain Bridgeman's ship, took the trouble of conveighing one of my letters to you; and since the date of that I sent you another by another vessel.

I hear Edward Thorn is arrived at Middleborough in Zealand. His mother, whom I have not seen in three years before, came to me some days ago, to enquire about her son. From me she went to the Exchange on the same errand, I having directed her to his correspondents. Some merchants, that are most concerned in the trade of those islands, give a very bad account of the manner of his coming off. I have endeavoured to justify him in that particular, upon what advice you gave me; though I cannot but think you were surprised at the suddainness of his departure; or else you would not have accepted of one hundred pounds security in so great a concern, especially having been admonished by frequent letters of the great hazard you ran by deferring the most important part of your business. I doubt you will hardly ever see him again in St. Christopher's Island, and I much question whether I shall ever see him in England. I hope, as you say, I shall receive more pleasing news from you, for the future, of my plantation affairs.

I am desired to put you upon an inquiry after a plantation, called Bettys Plantation in St. Christopher's Island near the Black Rock, late in the possession of one John Bettys; who it is that now has it; how he came by it; and, as near as you can, inform yourself of the title of it; whether Colonel Matthews seized it, and, if he did, for what reasons; and how he disposed of it; and whereabout the value of it may be. All which, I suppose, Lieutenant Munday can satisfie you in, or some old inhabitant. Let me know the particulars as soon as you can with convenience.

Your faithful friend,
CHRISTOPHERE JEAFFRESON.

Postscript.—I perceive, you writ to others,

tho' not to me, of the discovery you hoped you had made of a mine by my mountains.

Indigo is now worth gold; it is 4s. per lb.

LETTER CLII.
To Mr. Vickers, a planter in St. Christopher's Island.

London, 11 September, 1686.

You will have, I hope, received my letter by Mr. Duport before this can come to your hands, and, he having probably informed you of all concernes to the tyme of his departure, it would be superfluous to trouble you at this tyme with anything but what is of older date.

About a month ago, we had the news that Buda was taken, but it was soon contradicted; the truth of it being only that the Christians had lodged themselves upon the walls, but were not able to carry the town by assault, but continued upon the walls for above three weeks, having lost 4,000 men in the general assault; and when the Grand Vizier came to relieve it, the Duke of Lorraine drew out all his horse without the lines, and in some skermiges that happened between the advanced parties, that endeavoured to put men into the town, he had so great advantages over the Turks, that the Vizier thought it not convenient to hazard a battle, and the Christians, having received some recruits, resolved in a council of war to give another general assault; for that the basha of Buda was obstinate, and would hearken to no terms but those of a peace. He says the keys of Buda were the keys of Constantinople, and that he could not part with them but upon conditions of peace. The second instant (new style) the assault was given, the garrison being then reduced from 7,000 to 1,200. The basha was slayn, and many more in defending the breach. The Christians entered at their three attaques, and carried the town, putting all the men to the sword, excepting some few, who in the Round Tower in the Castle put out the white flag, and surrendered at discretion. This great action was the more considerable, as it was done almost in the sight of the

Ottoman army. The Christians have lost many thousands in this siege, in which they wanted nothing but good ingeniers. One Mr. Richard, an Englishman that was sent more to learn than to assist, was the best that they had. Several gentlemen of our nation have lost their lives in this siege; but this success is of so great consequence to Christendom, that the losses sustayned by it are to be forgotten. The two armies were so near that it will be difficult for the Turks to draw off without some farther action, of which the accompt is expected.

* * * * *

The Lady Stapleton is retourned; but to add to her sorrow, the French detain her three sons; and, unless our King will be pleased to demand them, they will not be permitted to come from the colledge where they are in the custody of men barbarously devout; who were so bloudy zealous, as to send the lady word they had rather stick a dagger to her sons' hearts, and see the blood of them, than that they should go with her to be bred hereticks (as they term it,) but the young baronet has the courage, that he tells them to their faces, if they keep him for eleven years there, he will never depart from his faith, which is great resolution for one of his age. Sir, I pray give my service to Mr. Dove and his lady, to your lady and sisters, and to Mr. Mead. With the tender of the same respect to yourself, I rest,

Your faithful servant,
CHRISTOPHER JEAFFRESON.

LETTER CLIII.

To Lieutenant Munday, a planter in St. Christopher's Island.

London, 16 September, 1686.

Lieutenant Munday.—You were pleased to intrust me a letter about four years ago, when I came off from St. Christopher's Isle to Mrs. Sarah Gordon, which I delivered with my own hands, according to the direction in Goodman's Fields; since which time the said Mrs. Gordon haith taken occasion to come to me several times at my lodgings, or where she could meet me to discourse me about her concerns in our Island, understanding I was a neighbour to her plantation.

She seems much dissatisfied; and I could not refuse this unthankful office, at her earnest request, to acquaint you how unkindly she takes it from you, that you do not make her due retourns of her rents and profits of her land accrewing and growing due to her, and that you do not give her a true and right understanding of the state and condition of her interest. For she knows not what is, and what is not let, or upon what termes; nor what is manured by yourself; for that she is informed that all the land is used, and yet she cannot tell what she may annually expect from it,—she being very desirous to be at a certainty.

I perceive she is so much disturbed in her mind about it, that if there be not some better complyance or more perfect understanding between you in some reasonable tyme, she will endeavour to sell or grant a new power to some other, or by some means seek for relief, in those respects where she looks upon herself aggrieved. And indeed, the clamour of such complaynts is so injurious to a man's reputation, that it is by all reasonable ways to be avoyded. I have all along given her what assurance I could from the knowledge I had of you. I told her that you have the character of a very honest, fair-dealing man, and I always esteemed you such. I told her of my sufferings of that nature, which have been very great, and which make me apt to commiserate any that seem to be fellow-sufferers with me. But I hope she has fallen into better hands. For I am confident that when you can procure freight on more reasonable terms, you will remove the cause of her complaynts, which as a friend I will advise you to do for your own sake. Assure yourself that what I do in this matter is not out of any ill-will to you. I could not refuse Mrs. Gordon's earnest desire that I would write to you, which I have done in plain terms, that you may know her mind. I am not fond of being concerned in other men's affairs. I find trouble enough of my own. But what I have undertaken at this tyme will be, I hope, so taken, that I shall be glad to hear from you; and you may be assured I ever valued you, and wished well to you. I pray you give my love to your wife and your daughters and sons, who, I hope are in good health.

CHRISTOPHER JEAFFRESON.

LETTER CLIV.

To Mr. Sedgewick, the Writer's Agent and Steward in St Christopher's Island.

London, 16 September, 1686.

Mr. Sedgewick.—I desire you to seal and deliver the enclosed, according to direction. Sir Nathaniel Johnson was this day upon the Exchange. He says that he shall begin his voyage about Christmas, and that his Majestie has given him liberty to choose which island he pleases to settle upon. I have not taken any freight, but have a promise from Captain Ganden that he will let you have some, if you have occasion for it, at market-price; and I desire, if you have any goods ready, that you would ship them by the first opportunity, whilst we have peace, and the seas are clear. For the rest, I refer you to my other letter, and am

  Your loving friend,

    CHRISTOPHER JEAFFRESON.

[In a letter to the same correspondent, dated 9 August, 1686, the writer had described Sir Nathaniel's alacrity in obtaining from the King, immediately on General Stapleton's death, a promise of the appointment for which he had waited some time : — " Sir Nathaniel carried the news to Windsor, and has gotten a grant of his place."— J. C. J.]

INDEX.

A.

Abraham, Francis, II., 196, 200.
Adam, Ellenor, II, 127.
Adams, Roger, II., 200.
Addy, Mr., II., 187.
Agent of St. Christopher's Island, negotiations for an, I., 239, 240.
Albemarle, Duke of, II., 219, 223, 224, 280, 302.
Allen, Mr., Obediah, I., 185.
American Dialect, I., 12, 13.
American Morality, I., 162, 163.
Amsterdam, Duke of Monmouth in, II., 147, 150.
Amsterdam, factious opposition to the Prince of Orange in, II., 110.
Andrews, Sir Edmund, II., 302.
Anglesey, Lord, II., 244.
Anne, Queen, I., 164.
Antigua, I., 180.
Aplon, Serjeant, I., 18.
Appearance of Charles the Second on the Sunday before his death, II., 174.
Argyll, Earl of, I., 154, II., 206. 217, 218.
Armstrong, Sir Thomas, II., 141.
Arnex, Jane, II., 200.
Arran, Lord, II., 266.
Arundel of Wardour, Lord, II., 304.
Ashley, Christopher, II., 127.
Aston, Sir William, II., 259.
Athol, Marquis of, II., 218.
Athy, Captain, II., 255.

Atkens, Chief Baron, II., 280.
Atlee, Charles, II., 126.
Atwood, Mr., barrister, II., 134.
Avery, Mr., I., 236, 249, 294.
Aylesbury, the Earl of, II., 222.
Ayliff, the rebel, II., 218.

B.

Baker, Mr., I., 227.
Banker, failure of a Lombard Street, II., 34.
Bantam Claims, II., 138, 148, 150.
Bantam, fall of, II., 51, 52.
Barnett, John, II, 126, 192.
Bartholomew, Captain, I., 300, 313.
Bath and Wells, Bishop of, II., 208.
Bathurst, Sir Benjamin, II., 272
Bateman, Charles, II., 134.
Banden, Mr., I., 318.
Baxter, Mr., I. 318. II., 98, 101, 125, 129, 134, 186, 215, 251, 298.
Bayer (or Byar) Colonel., I., 318. II., 5, 76, 255.
Beaufort, the Duke of, II., 220.
Belchamber, Mr. Thomas, II., 249, 258.
Benifield, Mr., I, 18.
Benninfield, John, II., 93.
Benningfield, Sir, Chief Justice of the Common Pleas, II., 280.
Berry, Captain, II., 54.
Bettys, John, II., 318.

INDEX.

Bewmingen Van, II., 138, 147, 149.
Billingsgate wharf, I., 67, 168.
Billop, Captain, I., 328, 329. II., 37, 74, 79, 157.
Binns, Robert, I., 18.
Blackburn, Mr., II., 117.
Blake, Captain, II., 39.
Blanarque, Count de, I., 98, 106, 108, 223, 245, 246. II., 256.
Blathwait, Mr. Secretary, I., 139, 140, 145, 150, 312, 320, 326, 327, 328. II., 24, 31, 32, 42, 44, 48, 59, 72, 76, 88, 98, 101, 112, 140, 151, 153, 162, 164, 203, 224, 256, 271, 301.
Bompstead, Stephen, II., 126.
Bond, Mr., I., 18.
Bond-servants in the West Indies, II., 299, 300.
Bonrepos, Monsieur, II., 283.
Boston, great fire of, I., 104, 244.
Bourne, John., II., 200.
Bowman, Captain, II., 35, 44.
Brandon, Lord Gerard of, II., 244, 250, 260.
Brecknell, Captain, II., 168.
Brett, Charles, I., 67, 101, 125, 126, 127, 168, 198, 217, 225, 249, 265, 274, 281, 294, 295, 313, 315.
Brett, Sir Edward, I., 149, 249. II., 96, 99, 104, 108.
Brett, Madam, I., 65, 108, 128, 133, 152, 225, 247, 274. II., 74, 107.
Brett, Major-General, I., 126, 226.
Brest, French fleet at, II., 188.
Bribes for a colonial secretary, II., 11, 12, 14, 15, 59, 101, 102.
Bridgeman, Captain, II., 85, 303, 313, 317.
Bridges, Mr. II., 167.
Brisbane, Mr. II., 19.

Bromfield, Christian, II., 200.
Bromley, Captain, I., 70, 180.
Browne, Sir Ambrose, Bart., of Beechworth Castle, I., 127, 226.
Bucaneers, characteristics and aims of the, I., 41, 42, 43, 44.
Buda, the siege and capture of, II., 149, 307, 308, 314, 319, 320.
Bull, Katherine, II., 93.
Bull Inn, the fall of the, II., 291, 298.
Butler, William, II., 200.

C.

Calhoun, William, I., 244, 245, 246, 247, 249.
Came, Captain, II., 284.
Camp on Hounslow Heath, II., 282, 289, 290, 297, 303, 304.
Catholic Chapel in Mincing lane, II., 285.
Canterbury, Archbishop of, II., 303.
Caribees, slaughter of, I., 39, 40, 41.
Carlisle, Captain Charles, II., 17, 33, 36.
Carlisle, James Hay, Earl of. I., 21, 85, 199.
Carpenter, Mr., II., 151, 249.
Carroll, Governor, I., 69, 180.
Cary (or Carry) Mr., II., 49, 58, 102, 116, 126, 306.
Case of the Bishop of London and the Ecclesiastical Commissioners, II., 307, 311, 312, 313.
Cavendish, Thomas, I., 7.
Channell Row, Westminster, I., 127, 128, 129, 130.
Chant, Captain, II., 185, 201, 279, 286.
Charles the First, I., 22, 32, 49, 101.
Charles the Second, I., 151,

154. II., 22, 23, 24, 37, 169, 177. Death of, 169, interment of, 177.
Charleton, Mr., II., 89.
Charleton, Sir Job, II., 280.
Cheeke, Captain, II., 33.
Chids, Mr., II., 316.
Chidley, Mr., II., 138.
Christopher, French Colony in island of St., I., 47, 48, 49, 50, 51, 52, 53, 107, 108, 204, 205, 213, 214, 215, 222, 223.
Christopher, Island of St., Plantation of, I., 17, 18, 19, 20, 21.
Churchill, Colonel, II., 219.
Churchill, Lord, II., 223, 224.
Clarendon, Lord, II., 245.
Clarke, Captain, I., 279, 298, 314.
Clarke, George, II., 200.
Clarke, Timothy, I., 250.
Clarke, William, II., 200.
Cleveland, Duchess of, II., 144.
Clutton, John, II., 200.
Codd, John, II., 126.
Codrington, General, I. 53.
Colleton, Sir Peter, I., 318. II., 5.
Compton, Sir Charles, II., 275.
Convicts, particulars respecting shipment of, II., 123, 124, 125, 126, 127.
Convicts, strange conduct of, II., 191, 192,
Conway, Lady, II., 275.
Cornish, sheriff, II., 134.
Coronation of James the Second, II., 182, 184, 188.
Cotterill, Catherine, II., 200.
Cottar, Colonel, I., 262.
Cotton, Sir Robert, II., 244, 250, 259.
Council Chamber, altercation in the, II., 44, 45, 46, 47.
Courteen, Sir William, I., 29.
Craven, Lord, II., 124.
Crispe, Captain, 1., 287. II., 84, 88, 98, 122, 139, 191, 201, 270, 306.

Crispe, Mr. Nicholas, II., 308.
Cronfield, Alice, II., 127.
Crook, Major, I., 201, 287.
Curley, Henry, II., 200.
Cushing, Captain, I., 279.

D.

Danby, Lord, II., 100.
Daniells, Sir Peter, II., 118.
Danvers, Colonel, II., 164.
Dartmouth, Lord, I., 141. II., 19, 29, 30, 32, 63, 72, 75, 82, 83, 89, 90, 110, 111, 265.
Dashwood, Sir Peter, II, 158.
Davis, Mr., II., 306.
Dayrell, Madam, I., 265.
Dayrell, Thomas, I., 305.
Deane, Colonel Richard, I., 57.
Deane, Sir William, I., 29.
Death and burial of Sir William Stapleton at Paris, II., 305, 315.
Death of Charles the Second, II., 169, 170, 174, 175.
De Grave, Peter, II., 214, 224.
Delamere, Lord, I., 156. II., 223, 244, 250, 258, 259, 260.
Delve, Serjeant, I., 85, 86, 199, 200.
Demure, Joseph, I., 255.
Den, Captain, II., 201.
Denmark, death of the Queen of, II., 184.
Denmark, Princess Anne of, II., 207, 212.
Descade, Island, I., 179.
D'Esnambuc, Mons, I., 49, 50, 52, 107.
D'Estrées, Admiral Count, I., 89, 98, 99, 106, 211, 212, 214, 216, 222, 223, 241. II., 182.
Detention of Lady Stapleton's sons in France, II., 321, 322.
Dorchester, Countess of, II., 261, 265, 269, 270.
Dove, Mr., I., 287. II., 251, 322.

Dover, Lord, II, 265, 304.
Drake, Francis, I., 6.
Duel in Covent Garden, II., 37.
Duel at Epsom between Captain Freeman of St. Kitt's and Mr. Freeman of Surrey, II., 304.
Duel at Newmarket, II., 53.
Duel between Mr. Compton and Mr. Seymour, II., 275.
Duel at Lambeth between Colonel Nethway and Captain Billop, II., 79.
Duel between the Duke of Grafton and Mr. Talbot, II., 275, 6.
Duel in a play-house, II., 144.
Duel without seconds, II., 83.
Dullingham Church, I., 3, 4.
Dunbarton, Lord, II., 144, 218, 221, 223.
Duport, Mr., II., 305, 307, 309, 317, 319.
Dupper, Sir Thomas, II., 166.
Durham, Bishop of, II., 260, 303.
Dusoe, Mary, II., 127.

E.

Edwards, Bryan, I., 25.
Elrington, Major, I., 287.
Ely, Bishop of, II., 208.
Embassies to foreign countries, II., 159.
Enchanted Island, the, I., 177.
Enos, Richard, II., 126, 200.
Essex, Earl of, II., 164.
Estcourt, Sir William, II., 154.
Evelyn, John, II., 19, 266, 269.
Execution of the Duke of Monmouth, II., 208, 209, 210, 211.
Explorers of the Sixteenth Century, I., 6, 7, 8.

F.

Farmer, Mr., II., 314.
Feneley, John, II., 134.
Ferguson, the rebel, II., 212.
Feversham, Earl of, I., 324. II., 112, 166, 187, 219, 221, 222, 224.
Fincham, William, II., 200.
Fire at Powys House, II., 144, 145.
Fitton, Mr., II., 207.
Flack, William, II., 126.
Fletcher, William, II., 127.
Fleet scattered in the Mediterranean, II., 110.
Floyd, Sir Phillip, I., 147. II., 46.
Ford, Richard, II., 126.
Foster, Captain James, II., 191, 195, 196, 198, 215, 216, 230, 235.
Fox, Mr., II., 84.
Fox, Mr., I., 287.
France, finances of, II., 97.
France, King of, II., 33, 49, 97, 110.
France, threatened combination against, II., 98.
Francis, John, II., 126.
Freeman, Captain, I., 202, 207, 209, 240. II., 31, 32, 63, 91, 198, 202, 304.
French Refugees, wretchedness and relief of, II., 294, 295, 296.
Frobisher, Martin, I., 7.
Frost Fair on the River Thames, I., 148 II., 103, 108.
Frugality of James the Second, II., 267.
Fuller, John, II., 200.
Funchial, description of, I., 174, 175, 176.
Fyson, Mr. William, I., 217, 262, 265, 302. II., 40.

G.

Gamiell, Colonel George, I., 63, 105, 149, 192, 210, 221, 237, 241, 243, 245. II., 96, 107,
Garbrant, Mr., I., 85, 199, 200.
Gauden, Captain, II., 325.
Gaunt, Elizabeth, II., 134.
Genoa, threatened with siege by the French, II., 162.

George, Lieutenant, I., 87, 105, 194.
George the First, I., 164.
George the Second, I., 101.
Gerard, Charles, Lord Gerard of Brandon, II., 223.
Gerard, Lord, of Gerard's Bromley, II., 150.
Germany, electors of, II., 98.
Germany, the Emperor of, II., 20.
Gibbon, Mr., II., 208.
Gibbs, Mr., II., 54.
Gibraltar, reported capture of, II., 82.
Gifts, orders prohibiting, II., 301.
Gilbert, Humphry, I., 6.
Glover, Mr., II., 37.
Godolphin, Lord, II., 150.
Goodenough, Richard, II., 223.
Goodman, Mr., the player, II., 143.
Gout, a remedy for the, II., 121.
Gordon, Mrs. Sarah, II., 322, 324.
Grafton, Duke of, II., 75, 144, 219, 275.
Grasscocke, Rowland, I., 18.
Graybridge, Lieutenant, I., 193.
Grays Inn, revels at, II., 10.
Greenfield, Mr., II., 54.
Grey of Werke, Lord, I., 156. II., 208, 211, 212, 222.
Griffith, James, II., 126.
Guadaloupe, I., 180.
Guards re-entering London on their return from the West, II., 211.

H.

Hackett, Sir James, II., 144.
Halifax, Lord, II., 46, 91, 147, 150, 266.
Halmaell, Mr. Van, II., 55.
Hambden, Mr., II., 104, 260.
Harden, James, II., 127.
Hardies, Mr., II , 46.
Hare, Captain, II., 300.
Hare, Colonel, I., 240.
Hare, Mr., II., 238.
Harrison, Ralph, II., 200.
Hart, Mr., II., 277.
Harwat, Matthew, II., 200.
Hawkins, John, I., 6.
Hay, James, Earl of Carlisle, I., 21, 22, 24, 28, 29, 32.
Hayes, Mr., II., 155.
Helmes, Captain, I., 300, 321, 324. II., 90.
Helmes, Mr. Robert, I., 181, 209, 220. II., 250, 258.
Helote, Mr., I , 86, 200.
Hemskerke, a Dutchman, I., 201.
Herron, Mr., I., 287. II., 273.
Hill, Colonel, Governor of St. Kitt's, I., 155, 159, 160, 161, 162, 299, 319, 321. II., 7, 9, 10, 11, 12, 15, 18, 20, 32, 44, 63, 100, 111, 112, 117, 118, 119, 121, 127, 129, 137, 142, 152, 165, 181, 184, 190, 191, 194, 204, 215, 227, 235, 241, 242, 248, 254, 271, 279, 292, 309.
Hill, Madam, II., 55, 228, 293.
Hobbs, Doctor, II , 55.
Holcroft, John, II., 8, 70, 71, 89, 132.
Holmes, Captain, II., 80.
Holmes, Sir Robert, I., 327, 328.
Holt, Sir John, II., 275, 280.
Hodges, Captain, I., 70, 180. II , 312.
Hone, Mr , II., 81.
Honours, rumours of intended bestowal of, II., 165.
Horse-guards, sickness and mortality of the, II., 183, 188.
Howard, Bernard, II , 244.
Howard, John, II., 127.
Howard, Sir Philip, II., 153, 156, 159.

Hughs, Sir William, II., 287.
Humiers, Marshal d', II., 82, 85.
Hunt, Mr., II., 171.

I.

Indigo, value of, I., 75.
Ingle, Captain, I., 286, 328.
Interlopers, II., 37, 38.

J.

Jackson, Mr., I., 133, 315. II., 128, 137.
James the First, I., 29.
James the Second, proclamation of, II., 170.
James the Second, II., 175.
Jeaffreson, Christopher, I., 3, 58, 63. II., 19.
Jeaffreson, Colonel John, of Dullingham House, Cambridgeshire, I, 3, 4, 5, 6, 17, 18, 20, 22, 23, 24, 25, 26, 27, 54, 57, 60, 85, 127, 197.
Jeaffreson, John, of Clopton, Suffolk, I., 60, 86, 126, 197, 228, 229, 302. II., 40, 51.
Jeaffreson, Joseph, I., 5.
Jeaffreson, Mary, I., 127, 226.
Jeaffreson, Robert, I., 200.
Jeaffreson, Captain Samuel, I., 5, 6, 26, 54, 199.
Jeffreys, Judge, II., 133, 134, 136, 144, 165, 258.
Jeffereys, Alderman, II., 255.
Jenkins, Sir Leoline, I., 145, 146, 147. II., 42, 43, 44, 46.
Jenner, Sir Thomas, II., 116, 118, 119, 142, 162, 163, 164, 182, 186, 275.
Jennings, Mr., II., 254.
Jessop, Mr., II., 86.
John, Mr. St., II., 154.
Johnson, Sir Nathaniel, II., 106, 110, 157, 166, 183, 310, 325, 326.
Jones, Serjeant, I., 18.
Jones, Chief Justice, II., 280.
Jory, Captain, II., 17, 18, 83.

K.

Ken, Dr., Bishop of Bath and Wells, II., 154.
Kennedy, Mr., II., 49.
Ketch, the executioner, II., 210.
Key, Joseph, II., 200.
Kirke, Colonel, II., 150, 153, 159.
Knights, Sir John, II., 88, 91, 98, 107.

L.

Lady of fortune, I., 115, 263.
Langford, Mr., I., 133, 315.
Langley, Mr., I., 18.
Lansdowne, Lord, II., 159.
Lashly, Mr., II., 37.
Luttee, Mr., II., 204, 268.
Lawrence, Captain John, II. 35, 36.
Lee, Mr., I., 305.
Legge, Colonel George, first Lord Dartmouth, II., 19.
Leigh, Sir Olive, I., 28.
Lestrange, Mr., II., 81.
Levins, Mr. Justice, II., 280.
Lewis, Mr., of Glamorganshire, I., 127, 128, 129, 152. II., 207, 288, 293.
Lewis, Madam, II., 149, 228.
Libels respecting the death of the Earl of Essex, II., 164, 165.
Liddal, Mr., I., 70, 180.
Lincke, Sir Thomas, II., 153, 156, 159.
List, Henry, II., 196, 200.
Lloyd, Sir Philip, II., 29.
London, Bishop of, I., 156. II., 260, 310, 312, 313, 316.
London, mortality and mourning in, II., 108.
Lorraine, Duke of, II., 149, 319.
Louis the Fourteenth, I., 49.
Loyal addresses to King and Duke, II., 119.

INDEX. 333

Lucy, Alderman, II., 255.

M.

Macclesfield, Lord, II., 207, 244.
Malefactors, discussion respecting, before the Lords for Trade, II., 163.
Malefactors, march of, I., 159.
Malefactors, negociations respecting, II., 102.
Marlborough, Earl of, I., 28.
Markam, Gervase, II., 287.
Marriage of a lady to a butler, II., 54, 55.
Marsh, Lady, II., 118.
Marshland, Mr., I., 198, 228, 303.
Martin, Captain, II., 254.
Martin, Mr., II., 303.
Matthews, Colonel, Governor of St. Kitt's, I., 89, 114, 117, 222, 246, 260, 263, 264. II., 318.
Matthews, Ensign, I., 325. II., 214, 223, 238, 265, 269, 271, 298.
Matthews, Madam, II., 54.
Matthews, Mr., I., 303. II., 5.
Mead, Mr.; I., 287. II., 249, 322.
Merifield, Ralphe, I., 16, 17, 19, 23, 24, 27.
Meux, Dr., Bishop of Winchester, II., 154.
Mews, the Horse-guards removed from the guard-house to the, II., 188.
Midleton, Gerard, II., 127.
Millett, Mr., I., 295.
Monk, Colonel George, I., 57.
Monmouth, Duke of, I., 154, 155, 156. II., 147, 149, 153, 208, 211, 212, 218, 219, 220, 221, 222, 225.
Montague, Chief Baron, II., 280.
Morgan, Mr., of Wales, I., 127.
Morgan, Dorcas, II., 200.

Morgan-ap-Hall, John, II., 200.
Morris, Silvan, II., 196, 200.
Morley, Dr., Bishop of Winchester, II., 154.
Morton, Colonel, I., 59, 60, 200, 201. II., 98.
Mounserrat, I., 180.
Mourning in London, prevalence of, II., 96.
Mulgrave, Lord, I., 311. II., 34, 265, 275.
Munday, Ensign, I., 287.
Munday, Lieutenant, II., 318, 322.
Murder of Sir William Estcourt at the Globe Tavern, II., 154.
Murray, Lord, II., 275.

N.

Navy, James the Second's address to the commanders of his, II., 302.
Needles, Mr., I., 170, 171, 178.
Nerrop, John, II., 200.
Nethway, Lieutenant-Colonel, II., 74, 79, 83, 85, 193.
Neville, Frances, I., 126, 226.
Neville, Sir Henry of Billingbeere, I., 126, 226.
Newmarket, fire at, II., 54.
Newton, Dr., II., 312.
Newton, Hugh, II., 287.
Nicolls, Captain, II., 279.
Nichols, Joan, II., 127.
Normanby, Marquises of, I., 311.
North, Captain Roger, I., 9, 14.
North, Roger, II., 133.
North, Lord Chief Justice, II., 6.
North, Lord Keeper, I., 158. II., 134, 136, 147, 153, 165.
Northampton, Lord, II., 275.
Northumberland, Duke of, II., 144, 153, 156, 159, 223.
Norwood, Captain, I., 268, 289.

O.

Oates, Titus, II., 134, 141.
Offley, Mr , II., 244, 259.
Oldish, Dr., II., 312.
Orange, Prince of, II., 82, 109, 138, 149, 245, 269.
Ormond, Duke of, II., 148, 150, 263.
Oxford, Earl of, II., 143, 219.

P.

Painton, Captain Thomas, I., 14, 15, 16.
Panden, Mr,, II., 102.
Papillion, Mr., II., 150.
Parkins (or Parkyns) Aden, I., 4, 182.
Parkins (or Parkyns) Colonel Isham, I., 4.
Parkins, (or Parkyns) Mary, I., 4, 57, 58, 60, 304.
Parkhurst, Mr., II., 290.
Parliament, preparations for, II., 179.
Parliament, liberality of the, to James, II., 243.
Partridge, Mr., I., 199.
Paule, Margarett, II., 127.
Parris, Mr., II., 316.
Peacock, Madam, I., 280, 305.
Pell, John, II., 200.
Pelly, Captain, II., 193, 249.
Pemberton, Sir Francis, I., 312.
Pemberton, Lord Chief Justice, II., 5.
Penney, Mr., I., 96, 134, 295. II., 43.
Percivall, Mr., I., 217, 265, 301. II., 40.
Perkins, Edward, II., 200.
Persecution of French Protestants, II., 245, 251, 254.
Peterborough, Lord, II., 144.
Petition from the writer to Charles the Second, II., 23.
Phippard, Captain, II., 170, 171, 172, 175,

Phipps, Sir Constantine, Lord Chancellor of Ireland, I., 61, 131, 132, 133, 310, 311, 312, 315. II. 29, 49, 60, 64, 79, 84, 91, 97, 113, 114, 128, 133, 134, 135, 147, 155, 171, 288, 316.
Phipps, Mrs. Constantine, II., 156.
Phipps, Mr. Francis, I., 133, 315.
Phipps, Captain, I., 61, 131, 132, 309, 310, 312. II., 9, 28, 53, 56, 60, 64, 71, 76, 80, 86, 92, 100, 105, 106, 112, 114, 115, 120, 128, 145, 154, 155, 161, 168, 201, 268, 270.
Phipps, Mr. Thomas, I., 133, 315.
Phipps, Mrs. Thomas I., 133.
Phipps, Sir William, I., 310.
Pickfourd, Mr., I., 185.
Pierce, William, II., 195.
Planters of the Seventeenth Century, I., 9, 10, 11.
Plott, Mr., II , 98, 99.
Pogson, Captain, I., 131, 287. II., 15, 31, 32, 37, 84, 86, 121, 202, 204, 268.
Poisoning, strange case of attempted, II., 144.
Poland, King of, II., 81.
Portsmouth, Duchess of, II., 140, 143, 150.
Portugal, the King of, I., 172, 173.
Potter, Mr., II., 144.
Powys, Lord, II., 144, 266, 304.
Poyntz, General, I., 67.
Poyntz, William, I., 66, 67, 75, 76, 83, 95, 102, 104, 111, 125, 152, 182, 190, 203, 204, 205, 206, 220, 229, 231, 232, 233, 243, 248, 249, 252, 254, 264, 265, 267, 295.
Price, Dr., II., 312.

INDEX.

Prichard, Sir William, II., 150.
Proclamation of James the Second, II., 170.
Protestants, persecution of French, II., 281.
Putney Heath, grand military review on, II., 143.

Q.

Queen's anger at the Countess of Dorchester, II., 265, 269.

R.

Radcliff, Mr., I., 287.
Raleigh, Walter, I., 6, 8.
Reade, Colonel, I., 69, 180.
Reade, Madam, I., 69.
Rebellion in the West of England, II., 218, 219, 220, 221, 222, 225, 226.
Rebellion in Scotland, II., 217, 218, 225.
Reed, Mr. Ben, II., 38.
Reeves, Mrs., II., 137.
Reeves, Mary, II., 200.
Restoration of White Staff officers, II., 177.
Rezio, Abraham, II., 268.
Rhodes, John, I., 18.
Richard, Mr., II., 321.
Richardson, Captain, I., 143, 145, 146, 147. II., 35, 36, 40, 41, 42, 44, 45, 46, 47, 48, 58, 122, 124, 185, 200.
Richelieu, Cardinal Duc de, I., 50.
Right, Mrs., II., 116.
Ring, William, II., 134.
Ripon, Dean of, II., 208.
Roberts, Captain, II., 178.
Rochester, Bishop of, II., 260, 303.
Rochester, Earl of, II., 148, 150, 165.
Rodeny, Captain, I., 287. II., 267, 284.
Rogers, Captain, I., 313.
Rogers, Mr., II., 55.
Romans, King of, II., 49.

Rosewell, Mr., Nonconformist preacher, II., 134, 144, 155.
Rotheram, Mr., barrister, II., 134.
Rough weather in the Channel, II., 270.
Rouse, Mr., II., 81.
Royal Progress into the West, II., 310.
Rumbold, the rebel, II., 218.
Russell, Colonel, I., 71, 114, 181.
Russell, Sir James, I., 114, 115, 262, 300. II., 18, 98, 106, 204, 215, 268, 270, 271.
Russell, Lady, II., 73, 85, 98, 106, 107.
Russell, Lord William, II., 81, 89.
Russell, Madam, I., 114, 115, 116, 117, 119, 120, 260, 262, 263, 270, 281, 299. II., 76, 204.
Ryle, William, I., 18.
Rye-House conspiracy, I., 151.
Rye-House Plot, Lords concerned in, II., 101.

S.

Sansbeck, a Dutchman, I., 214.
Saunders, Lord Chief Justice, II., 39.
Savoy, Duke of, II., 281.
Sawyer, Sir Robert, II., 133, 134, 135, 136, 147.
Saxton, the perjurer, II., 259.
Sea, extreme distress of a ship at, II., 109.
Sea, violent storms at, II., 148, 149.
Sedgewick, Mr., I., 164. II., 113, 146, 190, 191, 231, 234, 237, 245, 247, 251, 252, 263, 267, 277, 279, 286, 299, 325.
Sedley, Sir Charles, II., 266, 269.
Severine, Mr., II., 61.
Seymour, Mr., II., 275.
Shambray, Mr. Du, II., 31.

Sharp, Rev. Dr., I., 156. II., 310, 311, 316.
Shrewsbury, the Earl of, II., 276.
Sidney, Algernon, II., 89.
Size, Captain, II., 122, 123, 124, 125, 128, 157, 185, 187, 192, 216.
Slaves, negociations for the purchase of, II., 272, 273.
Small-pox raging in London, II., 96.
Smith, John, II., 126.
Smith, Mr., II., 216.
Smith, Thomas, II., 195, 200.
Smith, Sir William, II., 138.
Snow, Captain, II., 27.
Soames, Mr., II., 159.
Soldiers, procession of, II., 116.
Somerset, the Duke of, II., 290.
Sondon, Mr., II., 86.
Spaniards in the West Indies, I., 35, 36, 37, 38.
Stafford, Lord, II., 203.
Stamford, Lord, II., 223, 244.
Stapleton, Colonel, I., 243.
Stapleton, Lady, I., 77, 91, 114, 115, 196, 197, 262. II., 265, 271, 315, 321.
Stapleton, General Sir William, Bart., captain-general of the Leeward Islands, I., 71, 106, 114, 115, 123, 139, 140, 141, 150, 151, 195, 222, 240, 241, 243, 245, 251, 252, 321, 324, 326. II., 16, 61, 72, 76, 83, 88, 91, 98, 99, 110, 111, 117, 157, 167, 169, 198, 202, 204, 224, 231, 236, 241, 255, 265, 268, 269, 271, 281, 283, 298, 300, 304, 310, 315, 326.
State trials, Constantine Phipps's briefs in, II., 134, 155.
Steele, John, I., 287, 323. II., 62, 68, 69, 70, 87, 252.
Steele, Mrs., II., 87.
Stevenson, Thomas, II., 200.
Story, Mr., II., 149.

Sugar, value of, I., 75.
Sunderland, Lord, II., 160, 316.
Sunderland, Nathaniel, II., 127.
Surfet-Water, II., 69.
Swift, Dean, I., 310.
Sydley (Sedley) Madam, Countess of Dorchester, II., 261, 265, 269, 270.
Sydney, Algernon, II., 105.
Sympkin, Mr., I., 325. II., 49, 58, 102, 214, 268.

T.

Talbot, Mr., II., 276.
Tangier, reported demolition of, II., 89, 90.
Tasted, William, I., 18.
Tavern, sudden death of Lord Gerard in a, II., 150, 151.
Temple, Mr., the Lombard Street banker, I., 138. II., 32, 34.
Temple, William, II., 200.
Tennison, Dr., II , 208.
Thames frozen over, II., 103, 108.
Thames, scene on the, when Monmouth and Grey were brought prisoners to Whitehall, II., 208.
Thomson, Mr. I., 261.
Thorn, Ensign Edward, I., 91, 92, 94, 95, 96, 97, 102, 111, 112, 122, 134, 135, 136, 157, 229, 231, 244, 250, 253, 254, 282, 284, 285, 288, 293, 295, 307, 314, 315, 322. II., 3, 20, 26, 27, 35, 43, 50, 55, 56, 57, 58, 60, 61, 62, 63, 67, 68, 71, 72, 76, 77, 78, 84, 86, 87, 89, 90, 92, 93, 104, 105, 106, 112, 113, 114, 121, 129, 131, 139, 151, 154, 155, 171, 179, 189, 190, 227, 230, 231, 232, 233, 234, 236, 237, 238, 240, 242, 248, 252, 267, 274, 285, 317.
Thornbury, Colonel, II., 5.

INDEX. 337

Thoroughgood, John, II., 200.
Tippet, Mr., II., 86.
Tobago, battle of, I., 211, 212.
Tokens of friendship, I., 131, 132.
Token-drinking and token-feasting, custom of, I., 132, 133. II., 64, 306, 307.
Toledo, Don Frederick de, I., 55, 56, 57.
Toulon, seizure of English ships at, II., 167.
Townsend, Elizabeth, II., 200.
Tower, Lords in the, II., 223.
Trade in the seventeenth century to the West Indies, I., 75, 76, 77.
Trant, Patrick, I., 325, 326. 329. II., 167.
Treaty of Neutrality, the failure of negociations for a, I., 246, 247.
Treaty of Neutrality, II., 256, 257.
Trenchard, Mr., II., 206.
Trial of Lord Delamere in Westminster Hall, II., 258, 259.
Tulse, Sir Henry, II., 88, 91.
Turkey, grand-vizier of, II., 314, 319, 320.
Turkey, the tottering state of, II., 97.
Turks, great defeat of the, II., 86.
Turks, the Venetians combining with the Pope and Emperor against the, II., 104.
Tyrconnell, Lord, II., 266, 299, 303.
Tyrrell, Sir Timothy, II., 106, 107.

U.

Usher, Mr. Hezekiah, I., 188.

V.

Vanderveil, Master, I., 67, 169.
Vickars, Thomas, II., 200.

Vickers, Mr., I., 159, 160, 161, 287. II., 121, 125, 129, 164, 166, 187, 188, 189, 192, 193, 198, 232, 233, 240, 242, 248, 253, 274, 289, 319.
Vienna, the relief of, II., 81.
Voller, John, II., 126.
Voller, Robert, II., 126.
Voyse, Mary, II., 200.

W.

Wages in the West Indies, I., 79, 207, 208, 209.
Wallbanck, John, II., 200.
Walcote, Captain, II., 81.
Walgrave, Lord, II., 265.
Walker, John, II., 196, 200, 254.
Wallop, Mr., barrister, II., 134.
Wapping, a great fire at, II., 250.
War declared by the French King against the Dutch and Spaniards, II., 75.
War-panic in the West Indies, I., 97, 98, 99, 100, 221, 222, 223, 224.
Ware, Mr. I., 18.
Warner, Edward, I., 18.
Warner, Colonel, II., 92.
Warner, Sir Thomas, I., 5, 6, 9, 10, 13, 14, 16, 17, 18, 19, 20, 21, 22, 23, 24, 25, 26, 27, 28, 31, 32, 49, 55, 80, 107, 199, 225, 226. II., 55.
Warner, Mrs., I., 18.
Watkins, Jacob, II., 126, 235, 249.
Watkins, Mrs., I., 200.
Waugh, Serjeant, I., 298.
Weaver, Mr., I., 18.
Webb, Colonel, II., 154.
Webster, Captain, II., 292.
Wedding of Constantine Phipps and Sir Robert Sawyer's niece, II., 135, 136.
Wentworth, Lady Harriet, II., 209.
Westcote, Mr., II., 86.

Westecut, Mr., I., 287.
West Indies, war-panic in, I., 97, 98, 99, 100.
West Indies, narrative of a voyage to, I. 167, 168 to 181.
West Indies, trade in the, I., 183, 184, 185, 186, 190, 191, 196.
West Indies, wages in, I., 79, 207, 208, 209, 257.
West Indies, various kinds of emigrants to, I., 257, 258, 259.
West Indies, value of convict-labour in the, II., 3, 4, 6, 9, 10.
West Indies to London, length of a passage from the, II., 27.
West Indies, cruelty of a steward in the, II., 67, 69, 77.
Westminster School, severe masters at, II., 118.
Whealey, Robert, II., 126.
Wheeler, Sir Charles, II., 74.
Wheeler, Sir Francis, II., 206.
Wheeler, John, II., 127.
Whigs, dejection of, II., 140, 141.
Wickley Roger, II., 126.
Wilkes, Mr., I., 305.
Willett, Captain, I., 287, 315, 317, 324. II., 114, 154 175, 183, 189, 251, 261.
William the Third, I., 164.
Williams, Barbara, II., 200.
Williams, Colonel, II., 37.
Williams, Mr., barrister, II., 134, 135.
Williams, Thomas, II., 200.
Williams, the Duke of Monmouth's servant, II., 212.
Williams, William, II., 200.
Wimingen, treaty of, II., 107.
Windall, Madam, II., 76, 149, 165, 168, 188, 193, 261, 276, 283, 293, 314.
Wingfield, Sir Richard, I., 59.
Winter, Captain, I., 318. II., 268.
Winter, extraordinarily severe' II., 95.
Winthrop, John, of Groton, I., 9, 10, 11, 13.
Withens, Sir Francis, II., 133.
Worden, Colonel, II., 166, 187.
Worley, Mr., I., 66, 81, 82, 83, 86, 92, 187, 189, 192, 198, 210.
Worsley, Sir Henry, Bart., I., 226.
Worthing, Colonel, II., 75.
Wrayford, Mr., I., 131, 325. II., 49, 58, 172, 214, 306.

Y.

Yarway, Tertenants of, I., 60.
York, Duchess of, II., 85.
York, Duke of, I., 151, 324. II., 85, 112, 116, 119, 153, 156, 159, 165, 166.

THE END.

www.ingramcontent.com/pod-product-compliance
Lightning Source LLC
Chambersburg PA
CBHW030306240426
43673CB00040B/1079